In the Country of the Young

HARPER'S
MAGAZINE
PRESS

BOOKS BY JOHN W. ALDRIDGE

social commentary

> IN THE COUNTRY OF THE YOUNG

literary criticism

> AFTER THE LOST GENERATION
> IN SEARCH OF HERESY
> TIME TO MURDER AND CREATE

fiction

> THE PARTY AT CRANTON

edited works

> CRITIQUES AND ESSAYS ON MODERN FICTION
> DISCOVERY # 1
> SELECTED STORIES BY P. G. WODEHOUSE

In the Country
of the Young

by John W. Aldridge

A HARPER'S MAGAZINE PRESS BOOK
Published in Association with Harper & Row
New York, Evanston, and London

Portions of this work first appeared in *Harper's Magazine*.

To Alexis
your blood and mine

Preface

This book is a highly personal, highly impressionistic study of the younger generation in America in these years when the life-styles of the young—their manners, morals, and, above all, their militant social concerns—have so radically affected the cultural climate in which we live. I have departed from popular custom by presuming to suggest that the influence of the young is not always salutary, that their motives are not always above suspicion, that their values are not always impeccable, and that the fact of their youth does not by itself guarantee them a monopoly on the world's virtue.

By reasonable standards this hardly seems a spectacular heresy. We have always had a tradition in this country of questioning majority opinion, particularly when it becomes, or threatens to become, establishment opinion, if only to make certain that it does not harden into dogma destructive of independent thought. It seems to me obvious that the young, by virtue of their sheer numbers, vociferousness, and evident unanimity of vision, represent an establishment of particular force at the present time, that their majority opinion is indeed hardening into dogma, and that it is fast generating an atmosphere of claustrophobic pietism exactly antithetical to the one which the young, in their desire for total freedom, supposedly wish to create.

Pieties of whatever kind, when they begin to collect around any movement, ought in a healthy society to be constantly under scrutiny by the skeptical and irreverent, just as pomposities should always be vulnerable to the deflating thrust of satire. At the moment at least American society appears to have lost its satirical power; its sense of humor seems to have collapsed completely; and as a result, the pieties and pomposities of the youth movement have been allowed to exist very largely unchallenged. In fact, they have been so piously and pompously championed by so many adults who would normally be vigilant skeptics that we are quickly approaching a state of youth establishment complacency as offensive in its self-righteousness as any establishment of the extreme right or left.

In taking up the position of devil's advocate I perhaps should say that I have not been deliberately oblivious to those aspects of the youth movement which are clearly praiseworthy and socially valuable. I believe, for example, that the young are perfectly right to hate the Vietnam War and sincere in their wish to abolish poverty, prejudice, ignorance, injustice, and air pollution. But I have deliberately chosen not to emphasize the admirable features of their case because I wanted most of all to advance the case of critical skepticism by calling attention to those less admirable features which seem to me to have been ignored or glossed over by their many apologists.

In the Country of the Young

In particular, I have tried to counteract or at least soften the effect of that very vigorous and, to me, wholly fraudulent publicity campaign which in recent years has been devoted to selling the public on the idea that the current young are the most intelligent, sensitive, morally scrupulous, and generally magnificent generation ever to grace human history. In saying this, I realize that the young cannot be held responsible for the image of themselves which Madison Avenue has created. But they *can* be held responsible for believing it.

I am nevertheless well aware of the fact that there must be many of the young who do not believe it and who also do not fit the descriptions I offer here. Obviously, there are countless exceptions to any general statement one can make about a social group, and I doubt that it is possible to say anything about an entire generation which will represent the whole truth about them. But then I could not possibly aspire to tell the whole truth. I have tried, rather, to present what I believe to be *a* truth, a statement which will have some validity as a composite portrait of general traits and tendencies. And I would like to think that even though perhaps few young people will find themselves described here with total accuracy, there will be very few indeed who, if they are honest, will fail to find something in what I say that applies specifically to them.

John W. Aldridge

Ann Arbor, Michigan
November, 1969

In the Country of the Young

By the end of the sixties this country will have been dominated by children for almost twenty-five years. Ever since World War II the needs, values, styles, and demands of the young have been the major neurotic concern of very nearly the whole of our educated adult population. Our postwar passion to breed, which spawned the baby boom of the fifties, died, seemingly overnight, into a guilty preoccupation with our offspring, and this in turn has ended by making us peculiarly vulnerable to attack from the current armies of self-righteous puberty and dissident studentism. The result is that those of us who are now in our forties have scarcely known a moment in our mature lives when we have not been either changing diapers or under siege, when we have not been obliged to seek and shape our identities in the face of enormous moral and emotional pressure from the adolescent or preadolescent establishment. There may even be something more than paranoid truth in the thought that today the most vehement complaint of the young against us can be made with greater justice against them, that it is they who are now manipulating us, who are programing our minds to work within

alternatives which they *have invented, and forcing us to
conform to* their *authoritarian and bureaucratic plans for
the renovation of the modern world.*

*Certainly, young people have radically influenced,
where they have not positively dictated, our views on just
about every significant issue confronting us in this age.
We have been told by them what we had better think
about race relations, foreign policy, the problems of
backward nations, the war in Vietnam, the poor and
underprivileged, the industrial, military, and educational
hierarchies, marriage, sex, drugs, nudity, perversion, ob-
scenity, and pornography. They have created the prevailing fashions in manners, morals, dress, and personal
hygiene (or the lack of it), and have even given us new
standards of physical attractiveness based, it would seem,
on some new mutation in facial and body types which has
made their very persons structurally and physiognomi-
cally different from our own. They seem, for example, to
be the first generation which has succeeded in democ-
ratizing the human body and evolving a corporate type
or norm of female beauty and male handsomeness. Extreme variations in size, shape, and symmetry have been
largely eradicated among them. The face or figure whose
beauty is absolutely individual and unmistakable has
given way to a generalized young-class style which may
be appealing but is also highly forgettable. The ideal of*

good looks represented by the early Ingrid Bergman and Gary Cooper has disappeared so completely that when one sees those beautiful people on the Late Show, they seem like last survivors of some extinct superrace, as well as sad reminders of an age when a person could still be considered attractive after twenty-five. The new body style for men is neither tall nor short, fat nor thin. Classic Arrow Collar features have been replaced by the androgynous medieval squire or hairy simian look, ugliness now supposedly being suggestive of ferocious sexual vitality. Among male hippies this notion has been carried to the point where hair—usually of exactly the right color and texture—is worn like a pubic growth covering indiscriminately head, face, groin, and armpits, so that the entire person becomes a sex organ. For young women the latest fashion in face is a sort of fixed kewpie-doll vapidity. Cheeks are softly plump miniature babies' bottoms; eyes are like decorated Alfa Romeo headlights; and bodies appear to be transplants from promisingly contoured ten-year-old boys. Even the thighs exposed by miniskirts no longer seem to be the sexy upper parts of legs but interchangeable items of mannequin décor, purchased like wigs at boutiques.

By now the young have so intimidated us with the sheer clamorous weight of their physical and moral presence that some of us have almost been persuaded to

John W. Aldridge

---

believe that our primary obligation to society is to die as quickly as possible, so that they can inherit the earth without further delay. But even if we are not prepared to be quite this accommodating, we are forced to admit that the under-thirty generation, not merely as an age group but as a distinct social class, power structure, ideological movement, and supremely effective propaganda agency has been mainly responsible for creating the quality and mood of American life at the present time, and for making us feel that we belong to the most deprived and victimized of oppressed minorities.

If we ask how it happened that the young have managed to achieve such power over us, as well as how they happened to develop in precisely the ways they have, we might do worse than look for at least the beginnings of an answer to the way of life we created for ourselves and for them in this country right after the war. We might look, if we dare, at the world we made, and they are smug about having never made, back in the years when their values were being formed, and they were building their rebellious case against the values we seem to them to represent.

Part One

Part One

1.

Coming out of the war with long-deferred ambitions to live our lives, we settled down, began at once to breed, as if to prove we were still alive, and then proceeded to let our children do our living for us. It was a strange process, gradual, almost imperceptible, as natural as dying. Without quite intending it, we stopped—if we ever really began—making demands on life, perhaps because we thought there was no longer enough time for such frivolity, that our youth had been used up in the war, and that nothing must interfere now with the grimly earnest business of becoming middle-aged. Or it may be that the Depression and the war together accustomed us to asking nothing for ourselves, to seeing ourselves with a certain bleak pride as the sacrificial generation, to being grateful simply to have the necessities and utilities of existence. There was also the fact that the war had broken our connections with the past in a peculiarly final way. It represented a chasm separating not only two periods of time but two distinct cultural worlds. The social structures which had once ordered, contained, and given meaning to our lives—the structures of community, school, parents, relatives, and friends—had all been left behind on the other side of the chasm, and we had a powerful sense of being without identity or place, and an urge that was something near to panic to make a structure of home, wife, and children to replace what we had lost. So most of us put aside the brave plans we may once have had for adventure, discovery, travel, the book-lined garret for two in the Village, the trip to Hemingway's Paris, the novels, poems, and plays we had spent the war waiting to write, and we began to create a culture which was the perfect physical reflection of our impoverished expectations of life. And, not at all surprisingly, it resembled nothing so much as the military world we had just escaped.

From coast to coast we bulldozed the land into rubble, tore out the grass, uprooted the trees, and laid out thou-

4

sands and thousands of miles of company streets all lined with family-sized barracks. We turned forests and farmlands into mucky service areas and converted the rural outskirts of every major city and town into slurb-belt jungles of used-car lots, gas stations, hot dog stands, motels, army surplus stores, garbage dumps, and junk yards—our civilian equivalents of the honky-tonk and trinket-shop strips outside the army camps of Alabama and Texas. It was all ugly beyond belief and beyond bearing except to men who had become so environmentally desensitized by military life that they were no longer aware of their surroundings or could see no difference between the military environment and this one, simply because essentially there was no difference. The little square boxes of houses set in precise orderly rows could easily have been the married enlisted men's quarters at Fort Benning. The processed, powdered, concentrated, and frozen foods, the TV dinners, were the barest transition from emergency field rations K, C, and Ten in One. The shopping centers and supermarkets were simply enlarged PXs. And for this most domesticated of generations, a permanent condition of wartime impermanence was the central fact of life. Families were constantly moving from one housing development to another, like infantry replacements being endlessly transferred from camp to camp. And the atmosphere of military drabness and uniformity lay over everything. The houses, income levels, clothing, behavior patterns all seemed to be gov-

ernment issue. Even the children appeared to be interchangeable, as if their parents had drawn them at some
supply depot.

For children, of course, we had—were *all* we had.
Nothing else would grow in that atmosphere. We produced hordes of them, as if our only relation to Fortune
was to provide it with hostages. After a while, inevitably,
the children took over everything. They took over because there had never been an adult society here. There
had been only a physical structure of roofs and walls designed for one purpose—to afford us privacy for the act
of procreation and shelter for its teeming consequences.
None of us in these years seemed to have any sense of
the kind or quality of life we were trying to establish on
this barren ground, what our values were or our aesthetic
assumptions or our humane objectives. We had brought
no resources with us out of the past, no norms or prece-
dents of conduct, no tradition of amenities or graces,
luxuries or even comforts. We were like people who had
been deprived by disinheritance of the family fortune, the
heirlooms, the antique furniture, the silver service, the old
homestead. We had nothing to start with except our talent
for self-sacrifice, our compulsion to set up housekeeping
and live for the future of our children. So the children
rushed in to fill the vacuum, and with our full cooperation
and blessing they began to dictate the terms of our existence.

It became impossible for an adult to make a move—

if move he wanted to make—without taking them into account, without considering *them* first. If he took out the car, they had to go along. If he wanted to read a book or make love, they stomped and stampeded through the house and demanded their rights to his undivided attention. They arranged the schedule of meals and determined the hours when they would go to bed at night and their parents would get up in the morning. Educated and intelligent women gave up their lives fetching and carrying for them, playing with them, cleaning up after them, chauffeuring them to and from school, talking about them, worrying over whether they were getting the right food, the right vitamins, enough love and attention—and all because there was nothing else. We had created a huge corporate enterprise of promiscuous baby-making, and the other functions of life had to be set aside to keep it going. Also, it was an expensive enterprise, in both money and emotional energy. It seemed that everybody one knew was struggling, getting by, making do, doing it themselves, fretting over crab grass and leaky basements and new shoes for the three-year-old and the pediatrician's bills. There was no money and no time for adventure, excitement, or diversion. The children *were* our diversion, and what they diverted us from was the cold fact of our failure to conceive of life on any other terms or to ask for ourselves any larger rewards or richer experiences than those provided by parenthood. If we had pretensions to something better, they were necessarily

7

modest and mostly a matter of form. Gracious living for us was Chianti with dinner on Saturday nights and van Gogh prints on the beaverboards of the bathroom. But there were no resources for the cultivation of real style or taste or the development of anything like a civilized society. The social and cultural circumstances of life were those of a wall-to-wall ghetto. The houses were sleazy, cramped, joyless, and jerry-built, and even though they were crowded close against one another, the people in them did not connect or commune. If families in those years made a religion of togetherness, it was because there was nowhere else for them to be except together. Every house was an outpost in a wilderness of strangers, all seeking a cure for their loneliness by frantically reproducing themselves.

It is scarcely surprising that the offspring of this way of life, the beneficiaries of all this love and attention and self-sacrifice, should have grown up contemptuous of us or convinced that really we were dead all along and only they are alive. How could people be anything but dead or stupid or insane who had so little regard for their own needs, who asked so little for themselves? If we gave up our lives for them, it was only reasonable for them to suppose either that we did not value our lives or that they themselves must be terribly important to have provoked us to such fantastic generosity.

So we taught them by our example and by our obsequious treatment of them to have no consideration or respect for adults and a grotesquely inflated respect for themselves. We gave them a world which seemed to be designed exclusively for their pleasure and comfort, and yet which was impoverished in nearly all the resources necessary for the humane life, the adventurous life, the life of feeling and the life of thought. We gave them nothing to challenge or excite their imaginations except the environment of housing-development slums—an environment which, during their childhood and adolescence, came more and more to typify American life as a whole—and the only slightly more trivializing fantasy experience of television. As we grew in affluence and became even more permissive in an effort to atone for their steadily increasing estrangement from us, we bribed them with money to buy cars, clothes, popular records—the accessories of a purely materialistic, endlessly diversionary existence. And ultimately we subsidized their equally materialistic and diversionary rebellions against our materialism and affluence: their escapes into hippyism, in which they borrowed the costumery and bad manners of an outdated décor Bohemia; their experiments with drugs, in which they substituted the narcosis of psychedelics for our own narcosis of reproduction; their sorties into free-enterprise sex, in which at least they transferred the copulative scene from the stud farm back to the boudoir; their activist confrontations with university officials and campus police, in which at least they finally found an authority—indeed *in loco parentis*—that would put up resistance, however short-lived and ceremonial, and so provide them with an experience more real and psychically healthier than estrangement. If some of them wore the faces of crazed Bolshevik terrorists and the rags of Ganges penitents, at least they did not look sanitized, deodorized, depilatoried, and untouched by human hands. If they were arrogant and boorish, at least they were not melded into a *Good Housekeeping* blend of stalwart humility and pious liberalism. In short, at every step of the way they were fighting us, acting out a sad anti-parody of our sad burlesque of life. But the truly sad fact was that they became fixated in their stance of rebellion and, no matter how hard they fought, could conceive of no way of making us sufficiently formidable adversaries really to engage us, defeat us, and thus free themselves to become effectively adult.

Yet if we look behind the image of seemingly standardized behavior projected by the young, we become aware of paradoxes and contradictions which suggest that their actions derive not from a coherent ideology or even a coherent emotional attitude but more nearly resemble a series of random gestures enacted in a climate of metaphysical confusion. One notices, for example, that although they are passionate about causes and issues—especially as these relate to the quantitative, material problems of society—they are strangely indifferent to questions of quality, as well as to the processes of intellectual discrimination and analysis by which qualitative

10

judgments are made. It is as if the act of discriminating among qualities were inseparable in their minds from the act of discriminating among races, creeds, and colors, so that it has come to seem to them undemocratic even to think. Nevertheless, they can be ferociously hostile to the American way of life, to our bureaucratic political and economic structures, to the military and educational establishments, and yet scarcely be sensitive to the physical and cultural environment of America. They will demonstrate against our institutions, march on the Pentagon, fight in the siege of Chicago, and show only slight awareness of the ugly, ravaged, and littered no man's land in which they will be obliged to go on living aesthetically underprivileged lives even if all the institutions are overthrown and all minority groups have been liberated from poverty so that they can have a fair share in the collective underprivilege. One is struck, in short, by how philistine the young are in their idealism, how often their notions of reform are reducible to merely administrative and legislative action, the more equitable distribution of wealth, power, and opportunity, and how rarely they embrace measures which might be taken to establish in this country the social and aesthetic basis for a truly civilized society.

But the young are also remarkable for other inconsistencies: for their belief in progress and the perfectibility of man and their ignorance of, and indifference to, the lessons of history; for their insistence upon immediate

11

revolutionary reforms and their disregard of the inevitability of evolutionary process; for their interest in improving society and their evident determination to barbarize it; for their preoccupation with style and their boundless appetite for banality; for their moral severity and their personal scruffiness; for their indifference to standards of personal conduct when applied to them by adults, and their insistence upon the most exemplary standards of conduct when applied by them *to* adults; for their obsession with the nature and quality of university instruction and their disinterest in ideas, imaginative literature, and the values of the humanistic tradition; for their collective vociferousness and militancy of manner and their individual inarticulateness and limpness of manner; for their passion for individuality and their belief in collective action and group conformity; for their desire to "communicate" and "relate" to others and their apparent lack of substance to communicate; for their mystical belief in the primacy of intense feeling, the soul-rejuvenating benefits of fresh emotional experience, and their deep fear of uncertainty, contingency, and risk—all those situations of adventure and test which give the edge of fatality to life. Although they have more freedom of action, feeling, and opinion than any generation before them in our history, they are outraged by the existence of forces which in the slightest degree threaten to restrict or program or manipulate their responses. Yet if their dream of a problem-free society could ever be realized, it would very likely be a society in which the full horror of I.B.M.-card anonymity had descended, in which all human responses would be programed, probably at birth, the last hope of individual freedom or distinction erased by technocratic egalitarianism, and misfits and rebels, the scruffy, unwashed, and bizarrely costumed would most certainly be the first to perish under the sword.

To understand these confusions of attitude, we need to see them in the perspective of our national history as well as the specific history of the postwar period. If we consider first the question of the relative indifference of the young to the cultural environment and their almost exclusively quantitative and materialistic approach to the problems of society, I think it is obvious that both originate in the physical and psychological atmosphere that prevailed in this country in the fifties and early sixties. These years saw the rise on a mass scale of the kitsch-and-drek culture of the population explosion, as well as the emergence of a society committed to a belief in its ultimate perfectibility. The young were therefore brought up in an environment which, to preserve their sanity, they had to learn not to see, and in a moral climate in which it seemed that material measures could always be taken to eradicate material difficulties.

Their parents were, if they were typical, reasonably well-educated, liberal, and progressive believers in the power of positive manipulation and legislation. If conditions were bad, they could be changed through passing laws, signing petitions, working to elect enlightened poli-

ticians to office, supporting municipal bond issues, re-
structuring the local school board. In much the same
way, people with emotional problems could be manipulated by psychiatry toward accommodation and adjust-
ment; children with learning problems could be taught in
special classes; and children who were simply recalcitrant
or morose could be provided with a richer diet of diversion or extra helpings of love and attention. Means could
always be found to make certain that no one went hungry
or suffered injustice or felt insecure or depressed or
estranged. All that was necessary was the intelligent use
of the right techniques and the generous application of a
little *more* of everything to the affected areas. The aim, of
course, was to make life more orderly and pleasant, more
tolerant and democratic, and even perhaps more humane. But the effect was to make life more bland and
uniform, more disinfected of contingency, and more
deadening to the mind and spirit. For there was one
function which an environment of material ugliness controlled by a philosophy of material utility could not perform. It could not make life lovelier, more luxurious,
more adventurous, or more civilized. It was as if all that
was somehow beside the point or beyond the pale or too
expensive to contemplate or frivolous or contrary to the
principles of democracy—as indeed it was, since it depended upon the making of distinctions. But it was also
contrary to everything we had from the beginning learned
to expect life in America to be.

14

2.

The plain fact is that the basis for the civilized life—as distinct from the intellectual and the artistic life—has never existed in this country except briefly and almost, it seems, by accident at certain odd times and places in the past, such as colonial and nineteenth-century New England and the South before the Civil War. But the flowering of high culture in these areas was either too dependent on temporary regional conditions and declining European influences or simply too unvigorous to alter the utilitarian nature of the way of life which was spreading westward and would shortly fix the character of our national existence. By the time of the greatest influx of immigrants into the country, the transcendental and libertarian ideals of colonialism— the ideals of political and religious freedom, as well as the dream of an American Adam making a fresh start in a sinless New World paradise—had been largely replaced by a promise simply of unlimited opportunity to improve the material conditions of life, to be free not only to worship and vote as one wished but to become as rich and powerful as one's talents for exploitation would permit, without being held back by the restrictions of a social hierarchy or dependence upon the affluence of one's ancestors. Presumably, there was some slight suggestion in the immigrants' covenant with America that if material conditions could be improved sufficiently, the luxuries and graces would follow in the natural course of things. But the pioneers were not, for the most part, cultured men, and whatever vision of civilization they may have brought with them from Europe could not long survive in the rigorous life of the frontier. The sheer physical effort required to subdue the wilderness and provide the necessities of bare existence was such that no thought could be given to the problem of making life beautiful. But then, right at that point, something in our evolutionary mechanism went very wrong and has remained very wrong ever since. Logically, we should have evolved,

16

however slowly over the centuries, to the next phase of growth at which, with the close of the frontier and the spread of material abundance, a demand would arise for luxury and the cultivation of taste, intellect, and the social amenities. Instead, life in America became frozen —apparently for good—at the level of utilitarian existence. We somehow failed to advance beyond the point where we could provide the most physical conveniences for the greatest number of people. We simply went on providing more and more conveniences for greater and greater numbers of people. And, of course, with the passage of time these conveniences became increasingly efficient, practical, and necessary, as well as numerous and complex, so that before long the production of labor-saving devices and material facilities took the place of the resistant wilderness as the chief consumer of our pioneering energies. The hard work and ingenuity which had formerly gone into pushing back the physical frontier became diverted into pushing back the commodity frontier, into refining and endlessly re-refining the mechanical processes of life. In a very real sense, we have all along been engaged—and we continue to this day to be engaged —in a struggle to make this country fit for human habitation, and our existence within it bearable rather than civilized. Perhaps there is simply too much geographical space here, and physical conditions are too harsh, for us to feel that we have ever conquered our environment. So we remain arrested at the level of perpetual colonization.

That America is not yet a physically completed or settled country is everywhere so evident that just possibly it is too evident to be noticed. Certainly it is a fact we have had to do our best to ignore if we were to live with it at all. But virtually everything we, rather than God, have created here—except in the old areas of the original colonies—is stamped with the brand of the prairie and the frontier settlement. The typical main street of Anywhere-Nowhere, U.S.A., is still essentially that of a Montana cow town of the 1880s. The false fronts may be brick rather than wooden; the signs may be neon rather than painted; the saloons may have become cocktail lounges and the livery stables gas stations, but the effect is otherwise the same. It all has the appearance of having been thrown together in a great hurry to provide temporary shelter and the bare essentials of life for a people who are still in a migratory stage of development. We take it for granted that new houses will not be spacious or well-built or pleasant to look upon, that they will offer no luxury or ease beyond that provided by the average motel, that we can litter the countryside around them with all manner of industrial and commercial defecation. And we take this for granted because, even though we know better, the assumption is somehow built into us that the new houses will not be needed for very long, that settlements of still newer houses will be built further along the trail, and the people on the move will stay in them for a while before moving on again—moving always through

18

a landscape which we secretly recognize to be expend-
able, which is already so far gone in ugliness that it can
hardly matter if it is made still uglier. Like an eternally
advancing army, Americans have grown accustomed to
leaving their garbage wherever they happen to drop it.
They cannot take pride in an environment which looks to
them like enemy territory, and it is part of their national
heritage to suppose that they will never stay in one place
long enough to be obliged to police the area and bury
their beer cans.

The experience of driving by car from coast to coast is
a case in point. The very physical structure of the drive
is illustrative of our sense that the environment we are
passing through is not only not worth looking at but is as
alien to us as the wilderness must have seemed to the
first pioneers. The whole requirement imposed by the
superhighway system is that we drive as fast as we dare
and for as long as we can stand the strain to get where
we are going as quickly as possible. No provision is made
for dawdling, sightseeing, or exploring side roads or picturesque villages, if any were to be found. In fact, there
is a distinct implication that to leave the highway is dangerous, a descent into a hostile world of aborigines and
savage beasts, and that to enter it is to risk never being
heard of again. Everything seems to be arranged to make
very certain that one will not have an *experience* of travel
of any kind, that absolutely nothing will happen except
perhaps a blowout or, at the very worst, a collision with

another car. Motels and filling stations are so located that one need never venture beyond the immediate vicinity of the highway to refuel or spend the night. The chains of roadside restaurants are obviously not intended to be places where food and drink are tasted and enjoyed but rather way stations where people are provisioned like caravans or safaris with the bare increments of nourishment required to keep them alive until they reach their destination. Destination is the lone reality in the vacuum of such travel. We always move, it seems, both physically and philosophically through a present we do not care to experience toward some future time and place at which real life will finally begin. Like Gatsby, we are all believers in the green light, the orgiastic future—not only the young and idealistic but all of us. And a principal reason we are is that the physical world we inhabit from day to day affords us so few grounds for satisfaction and such abundant grounds for believing that tomorrow cannot help but be better.

In any case, it is no wonder that each new generation of Americans appears to be more anesthetized to the environment than the last, or that we seem able to survive within it only by making lairs or fortresses of our homes and staying inside them as much as possible. We are the most housebound and house-proud of nations, because there is so little worth leaving the house for. This is what the visiting European notices first about us: that we have no place to go except home. With all our preoccupation with facilities, we have somehow failed to provide any that would make our surroundings attractive or that would tempt us to move out into them and live attractively with one another. It may be banal to say that we suffer from having no village life or pub life or café life or market-square life, but we do. It is because we lack these things that our social life is so mechanical and perfunctory, so deficient in warmth and spontaneity. People do not just happen to come together here or decide on impulse to drop in on one another. They are *imported* into each other's houses after the host and hostess have formally placed an order for them well in advance of the desired date of delivery. When they arrive, the whole effort of hospitality is to get them drunk as quickly as possible so that they will soon not notice or care that they have nothing to say to one another. A social life, to be vital, depends upon the ability of a people to move freely and familiarly through their physical environment, to feel at home in it, and also to feel an organic connection between its character and appearance and their own human qualities and desires. It is no accident that the primitive mind identified the processes of the natural world with those of man and did not distinguish between the king and his kingdom. Some such sense of coherence would seem to be necessary before we can affirm our place in the communal order. But because we see our environment as alien and ugly, we inevitably feel estranged both from ourselves and from other people. For the psychological

habit of holding oneself aloof from uncongenial surroundings becomes a habit of social relations. To the extent that our surroundings seem remote and unreal, our
friends will seem remote and unreal, and to the extent
that we lack facilities for natural and spontaneous relationships with others, those relationships will become
institutionalized into empty rituals of conviviality and
merely histrionic gestures of intimacy.

Perhaps it is true that there has really never been very
much to do in this country except work. During the
period of colonization, idleness may have been a threat to
the developing economy, a breach of communal faith,
and a sin against God. But the Protestant work ethic is
the outgrowth of more than material necessity or religious
belief. It is also a moral imperative designed to compensate for a social deprivation. We have worked in order to
distract ourselves from the fact that there are so few resources here for productive and satisfying leisure. In the
process, we have managed to get an impressive amount
of work done, and we have created a whole society which
is apparently able to go on forever distracting itself with
objects and contrivances. We have made ourselves efficient, practical, and successful in order to survive in a
culture of humanly impoverished affluence.

3.

It follows logically—although the logic is poignant—that whenever we have tried to solve the social problems created by life in an alien environment, we have applied to them the same utilitarian methods which have helped to distract us from life in an alien environment. Now that the work ethic, rigorously enforced, has enabled us to close the physical frontier and push back the commodity frontier seemingly to its outermost limits, we have for some years been using it to push back the social frontier. Social engineering has replaced pioneering and profiteering as America's chief contribution to world progress, and our national self-image has become increasingly that of a country which, having succeeded in subordinating environmental phenomena to the material needs of men, is fast reducing men to the condition of environmental phenomena. This, in fact, has been the great evolutionary development of the postwar period: the shift of our technological interest from the conquest of things to the conquest of people as things. In the process we have, of course, employed the same materialistic philosophy that has served us so well in the past. If we brought a species of civilization to the wilderness by equipping it with mechanical facilities and conveniences, it has seemed to us perfectly feasible that we could engineer the salvation of society by making a wider distribution of these facilities at all levels of the social wilderness—as always, in the religiously utilitarian belief that quantities must sooner or later beget qualities and that goods and gadgets will provide the basis for the civilized life as well as rehumanize the dehumanized.

Social engineering is, of course, the inevitable response of technology to the social conditions of the modern American superstate. But it is also the expression of our growing estrangement from the social realities in which those conditions objectively and concretely exist. At one time, we would not have needed an elaborate complex of bureaucratic institutions to remind us that we inhabit a world in which the problems of others have some meaning in relation to ourselves. Daily experience would have provided us with an infinite number of occasions for human contact to confirm our sense of the reality of others and of our own reality among others. Most of us grew up enjoying the luxury of the microcosmic relation to society, of having an understood place in the small provincial worlds of family, neighborhood, town, or region, from which we derived and generalized our image of society as a whole. People of whatever variety or sameness of type were always identifiable as individuals whose ways and often whose histories were familiar to us, and the mass could always be imagined as simply a larger denomination of the local group.

But the population explosion and the collapse of the old communal structures have forced upon us a radically altered social metaphysics. As the possibilities for individually experiencing others have receded, we have had no choice but to begin visualizing society in abstract and macrocosmic terms, no longer as a reality accessible to us but as a vastly remote monolithic enterprise to which we necessarily relate more and more provisionally and programatically. By degrees we have fallen into the habit of seeing people as statistical phenomena or as a race of generalized others who do not exist except as embodiments of the inequities or injustices which first called them to our attention. And even as we offer them our official sympathies and register our concern for their predicament by writing our congressmen and supporting our favorite charities, we have to admit that we have lost the power to offer them the *felt* sympathies—or even, for that matter, the felt hostilities—we would automatically be able to give if they were real to us as persons. This is the great castrating dilemma of the American middle-class liberal. His humanitarian ideals derive little or no support from his human impulses. He is always forcing himself to love large masses of people he does not and cannot know, and would almost certainly dislike if he did know. He exists in a cultural situation which not only isolates him from the objects of his professed compassion but makes him incapable of sustaining the compassion he professes, if only because compassion felt for large masses of people who cannot be engaged as individuals must soon ossify into a mere stance of pious feeling. Hence our bureaucratic gestures of liberal humanitarian-ism—the distribution of welfare funds, the enactment of benevolent legislation—might be cynically interpreted as our ways of compensating the underprivileged for our failure to feel more than guilty about them. But these same gestures may also be our ways of making certain that our debt to the underprivileged will be discharged on terms that correctly symbolize the remote character of their relation to us, with the handout of goods, facilities, and money.

This is to suggest that the charitable measures we have taken and the institutional apparatus we have constructed to deal with the problem of social inequities in this country are finally the index of our social abstractedness —and not only our abstractedness from one another but from the environment as a whole. For just as we are unable to engage the reality of people who are habitually seen as social problems, so we cannot engage a social environment which is no longer a concrete medium for experiencing others but is rather a seemingly theoretical construct of conditions to be investigated, analyzed, and corrected. If the anesthesia of work is our mode of escape from the unpleasantness of life in an alien physical environment, the anesthesia of social engineering is our mode of escape from the impersonality of life in a social environment populated by aliens.

This same quality of abstractedness—and the corresponding need to compensate for it through a preoccupation with "facilities"—also typifies our relation to the artistic and intellectual life in America. For a good many years now we have sought, by means as artificial as irrigation ditches, to make high culture take root and flourish in our national desert. We have spent millions of dollars building museums, art centers, concert halls, and little theatres—to say nothing of colleges and universities —in most of the major cities and not a few of the major cow towns and cornfields throughout the country. We pride ourselves on having produced, for the first time in our history, a mass society composed of a sufficiently large number of educated people to have made culture

a leading industry, as well as very probably the chief
source of élitist values in the new leisure-oriented economy. If in fact there is a caste system in America today,
it is one based upon the knowledgeable and conspicuous
consumption of cultural products. Yet even though we
have been able to package and distribute these products
with all the expertise we normally devote to the sale of
household appliances, we have still not managed to give
culture an organic relation to the total environment. In
spite of the proliferation of cultural facilities, their
presence among us remains a phenomenon notable for
the violence of its contrast with the tone and quality of
the prevailing way of life.

It may even be that we are so thoroughly used to the
idea that culture is something superimposed upon or
imported into our society that we would be terribly dis-
appointed if it turned out to have some indigenous connection with it. Culture for us is still, regardless of our
official passion for it, essentially a diversion from, rather
than a vital expression of, real life. It may be something
we appreciate, perhaps even love, or that we consume for
status reasons or wear like costume jewelry. But it continues to occupy in our minds that category of abstract
and otherworldly entities like God, mother, and the Stars
and Stripes which we feel pious about and pay periodic
homage to but which we know perfectly well have little
or nothing to do with the concrete business of existence.

In this respect, of course, we are being beautifully and

consistently American and simply reasserting the moral schizophrenia of our ancestors. For it has all along been characteristic of American thought that it operates on two levels at the same time without any apparent sense of contradiction. Traditionally, we have believed—or pretended to believe—one thing and done another: preached transcendental values and pursued materialistic goals, paid lip service to the doctrine of doing unto others and constructed an economy based on the principle of doing others in, sung "America the Beautiful" and labored to make America ugly. So it is not surprising that our sense of cultural values should exist on a different level of consciousness from our sense of the practical realities, or that our approach to culture should be more utilitarian than aesthetic.

Nevertheless, it is one of the nicer ironies, and no more than we deserve, that our actual physical experience of culture precisely symbolizes our philosophical view of it. We have come to accept as a matter of course the fairly astonishing fact that our great cultural and educational institutions—scattered, as most of them are, here and there across the country—will almost always be totally incongruous with their physical surroundings, and that what happens to us once we are inside them will have nothing to do with what happens to us outside them. In this sense, all Americans, simply by virtue of having grown up here, have been conditioned from birth to a discontinuous and disharmonious relationship not only with cultural experience but with experience in general. Our environmental antennae are so constructed that they accept without a whisper of static the consecutive or linear accretion of phenomena, in which *this* occurs, and then *this* occurs, and then *this* occurs, with each happening encased in its own plastic bubble of reality forever separated from every other. Thus our social life has no relation to the life we lead when we are not formally seeing people; our professional or business life does not connect with our personal life; and our cultural life does not connect with our experience of the physical environment.

This is, of course, dramatically not the case in Europe where cultural institutions have evolved over the centuries out of a distinctive pattern of life and are the natural expressions of a particular quality of environment, which is in turn the natural expression of the quality of life of the people. In England, for instance, one may go to a concert of eighteenth-century music and walk out of the concert hall into a world of eighteenth-century architecture. Or one can attend university lectures on the Romantic Poets in rural surroundings of precisely the natural beauty that produced the Romantic Poets.

Americans, on the other hand, are accustomed to consuming their culture in islanded meccas of preposterous elegance set down in an environment of unspeakable ugliness. Or they will attend university lectures on the Romantic Poets in rural surroundings that could only have produced Grant Wood and the Future Farmers of

America. It is not at all unusual for us to drive for miles through a slurb landscape of Howard Johnson's, Jiffy Jumbo Burgers, Tastee-Freez, Piggly Wiggly, Totter-Inn, Etta's Clam Palace, Roger's Soul Food Eat-O-Rena, and the World's Largest Evangelical FM Station (Sacred Stereo) to attend a performance of Marlowe's *Doctor Faustus* in a civic center decorated with a variety of European marbles in colors ranging from pale peach to dahlia blue, elaborate chandeliers sweating with crystal, huge arched leaded windows, deep-toned plush-velvet carpets, massive sweeping staircases, and Edwardian palm trees encircled by tapestried love seats. At the end of the performance—which, more often than not, will be of excellent quality—we will leave behind this antic seraglio and drive back through those miles and those horrors without being troubled by any sense of incongruity whatever. And indeed perhaps we should not be, considering that the landscape and the kitsch décor of the theatre belong to the same world and are both equally irrelevant to the experience of the play itself.

The problem is, of course, that modern America is physically a proletarian world and the perfect embodiment of the philosophy that we were put on earth to work hard and not to live well. Our physical environment was created to meet the material needs of large masses of people who were either laboring men or who shared the tastes of laboring men. Hence life in this country imposes no aesthetic hardship on that part of the population who,

31

regardless of how well educated they may be in a formal way, have the sensory equipment of peasants or early learned how to look at their surroundings without seeing them. But for the person quirky enough to be environmentally sensitive, life here can be a nightmare from which he is much too awake to awaken, an experience of visual trauma so profound that life on the moon would seem a godsend to him, if only because it would be merely bleak. He is obliged to exist in a society formed physically on values radically opposed to his own, and constantly erosive of his own, and while this may be a stimulus to the production of rebellious art—as our intellectual history proves it to be—it is a serious obstacle to the pursuit of the civilized life.

It might be objected that for such a person there now exist abundant facilities, on a scale hitherto unknown, for the satisfaction of his cultural interests, and that, compared to the situation today, American life of fifty or a hundred years ago was as barren of cultural opportunities as the Gobi Desert. But we should also remember that if we had fewer of those opportunities a hundred years ago, we also had no mass cultural life as we now know it and far less uglification of the physical environment. It may have been harder in the past to find art galleries or concert halls unless one traveled to New York or Boston. But, once found, they could be enjoyed in relative freedom from the abrading proximity of the industrial jungle—and enjoyed most probably in surroundings of some real congruity with the aesthetic experience to be had in them.

The difficulty underlying the proliferation of cultural facilities in the postwar period, as well as the dramatic increase in the size of the educated public, is that uglification has also proliferated at a frightening and seemingly uncontrollable rate. We may have more art galleries and concert halls than ever before, and more people capable of appreciating them, but we also have more areas of urban wasteland and suburban slums. Hence the contrast has deepened to the point of hopeless disjuncture between the amenities provided for the educated minority and the environmental context in which those amenities must be enjoyed. In spite of our present high level of sophistication and taste, we have still not developed, and seem unlikely ever to develop, an aristocracy of taste sufficiently influential to improve to any important extent the quality of our physical existence. It was just such an aristocracy, reinforced by monarchical rule and enormous wealth, that created the cultural institutions of Europe and that civilized and humanized the total way of life of Europe, making it impossible, at least in certain countries, to distinguish between the landscape produced by high culture and the environment in general. Rome, for example, very largely *is* the accumulated art and architecture of the ages, and so, in differing degrees, are London and Paris. But the best we have been able to do is bring about a most tentative accommodation of our minority cultural interests in a cultural landscape vastly inhospitable to them. We have not been able even to conceive of a life of taste or civilization that can be pursued within the terms of the whole society—unless we happen to live in one of the scattered outposts of higher learning or in one of the great cities of the East and West Coasts, where we tend after a while to fall into the error of assuming that the strong cultural interests of the local society reflect those of the country at large.

What is true, furthermore, of the cultural life in particular is also true of those other interests and satisfactions which at one time were inseparable from the cultural life. Although we have seen since the war an improvement of the general taste which seems to parallel the increase in the number of cultural facilities, it is still necessary to say that once outside the major cities, one moves in a landscape of working-class tastes and amenities. Almost anywhere on the route between New York and San Francisco food and shelter are plentifully available at the lunchroom and Y.M.C.A. level. But if one wants something better, one is out of luck. Even allowing for the fact that conditions are not as bad as they used to be, it remains virtually impossible, again outside the major cities, to buy a really fine meal at any price or spend the night in a really fine hotel or travel by public conveyance anywhere in the country in really comfortable, let alone luxurious, circumstances.

Perhaps such things do not and ought not to matter

very much, particularly since we scarcely view travel, at least in our own country, as an experience to be enjoyed. On the other hand, they are not altogether frivolous considerations. The enjoyment of a fine meal or a night in a fine hotel may be a sensual satisfaction but it is also an aesthetic one. It is quite simply good for the soul, and it makes a man ever so slightly more human. It may even be not wholly preposterous to say that a satisfaction of this kind can have an important effect on one's continuing ability to perceive qualities and make distinctions and thus to hold out a little longer against the debasement of humane values which is occurring everywhere at the present time. We need to be reminded periodically that excellence is something more than an ideal of abstraction, that it is actually available, whether in the form of food and lodging or of aesthetic and intellectual qualities. We may be morally bound to give up our luxuries—or even to argue against the very idea of luxuries—in order to help the underprivileged win their fight for a fair share of the necessities. But it would be morally disastrous to live in a world in which luxuries were no longer available to anyone, rich or poor, and we gradually forgot that they ever existed, along with the civilizing standards which their existence once implied.

4.

This whole question of the quality of American life has been a major concern of our writers and intellectuals for almost as long as there has been an American literature. James Fenimore Cooper, Hawthorne, Mark Twain, and Henry James were all, in their differing ways, preoccupied with it, especially as it affected the kind and quality of art which America, in comparison with Europe, might be expected to produce. As far back as 1828, Cooper was complaining that one of the most crippling problems facing the writer here is sheer "poverty of materials." "There is scarcely an ore which contributes to the wealth of the author that is found, here, in veins as rich as in Europe. There are no annals for the historian; no follies (beyond the most vulgar and commonplace) for the satirist; no manners for the dramatist; no obscure fictions for the writer of romance . . . nor any of the rich auxiliaries of poetry . . . no costume for the peasant . . . no wig for the judge, no baton for the general, no diadem for the magistrate."

Thirty years later, Hawthorne made substantially these same charges in his preface to *The Marble Faun,* where he speaks of the difficulty of "writing a romance about a country where there is no shadow, no antiquity, no mystery, no picturesque and gloomy wrong, nor anything but a commonplace prosperity, in broad and simple daylight, as is happily the case with our dear native land." And James, in his little book on Hawthorne, echoes these statements and adds some extravagances of his own in his famous list of the socially given materials for literature which are available in Europe but sadly missing from the American scene: "No State, in the European sense of the word, and indeed barely a specific national name. No sovereign, no court, no personal loyalty, no aristocracy, no church, no clergy, no army, no diplomatic service, no country gentlemen, no palaces, no castles, nor manors, nor old country houses, nor parsonages, nor thatched cottages, nor ivied ruins; no cathedrals, nor abbeys, nor little Norman churches . . . no Oxford, nor Eton, nor Harrow . . ." And at the end of this epic catalogue the partly, but only partly, self-derisive touch of absurdity: "no Epsom nor Ascot!"

For these writers, the problem of the quality of American life was, as I have suggested, primarily an aesthetic one, a question of whether or not the native experience was rich enough and complex enough to provide the materials for a vital literature. But because of their infatuation with European culture and their ability to move more or less freely between Europe and America and exploit the artistic possibilities of both, one feels that, except in the case of James, their concern was to a very large extent theoretical and academic. Finally, it seems to have been a matter of trying to impose on American experience a conception of the novel which was not relevant to it and which had less to do with the actual quality of that experience than with the presence or absence in America of materials that could be used in the writing of the European-style novel of manners and the historical romance.

For some of their successors, however, and particularly for the writers who came to maturity around fifty years ago and who were exposed to the cultural deficiencies of America in a way that Hawthorne and James never were, the question of quality took a rather different form, became more personal and practical and therefore considerably more urgent: not simply whether the native experience could sustain a vital literature of whatever kind, but whether it could sustain a vital life, whether it was sufficiently civilized to satisfy the needs of men of real taste and sensibility. The answer given over and over again in the work of these writers is overwhelmingly negative. In fact, the defining feature of the literature which they, and those younger than themselves, produced, and the feature which, above all, defines it as a remarkably cohesive literature, is its attitude of profound dissatisfaction with the conditions of life in this country.

H. L. Mencken was the most articulate spokesman for this attitude, the most aggressive defender of the cause of enlightenment in what he consistently saw as a culture of hypocrisy, anti-intellectualism, and aesthetic starvation. But there were others such as **Van Wyck Brooks, George Jean Nathan, Randolph Bourne, Ezra Pound, Lewis Mumford, Waldo Frank,** and **Harold Stearns,** as well as novelists like **Dreiser, Sherwood Anderson,** and **Sinclair Lewis,** who either shared Mencken's views or were making critical pronouncements closely similar to his. And what seems remarkable today is that the enlightened members of at least one, if not two, entire American generations—whether or not they were practicing writers themselves—formed their conception of the state of the national culture or unculture almost exclusively on the work of these men. No other single body of opinion was so influential in shaping the character and tone of the intellectual atmosphere that prevailed in this country from roughly the beginning of the First World War to the middle of the thirties.

Those years produced work after work of sustained and vociferous indictment of the American scene: Lewis's *Main Street, Babbitt,* and *Arrowsmith;* Anderson's *Winesburg, Ohio;* Dreiser's *An American Tragedy;* Brooks's *America's Coming-of-Age;* Stearns's symposium *Civilization in the United States* (which provided the ideological basis for the expatriate movement); Dos Passos's *Manhattan Transfer* and *U.S.A.;* and even the novels of Scott Fitzgerald, which may seem to begin, and in a sense do begin, as celebrations of American life but contain an implicit criticism of our manners and values finally as devastating as any to be found in our literature. From 1924 to 1934, during the editorship of Mencken and Nathan, the *American Mercury* carried on a continuous campaign against everything it saw to be fraudulent, gauche, stupid, and ugly in this vast nincompoop republic, and the *American Mercury* became the bible of the sophisticated and disenchanted of every age and class.

In his essay "On Being an American," Mencken made a statement which was typical of him and of the attitude he and his magazine helped to popularize. "The United States," he said, "is essentially a commonwealth of third-rate men . . . distinction is easy here because the level of culture, of information, of taste and judgment, of ordinary competence is so low." For him the problem

40

was clear and simple, perhaps in our view much too clear and simple. The major threat to the civilized life in America was philistinism, the tyranny of the mob or mobocracy, the proliferation, particularly in the Midwestern hinterlands, of that cretinous subspecies which he called *boobus Americanus.* Yet however quaint or blustering Mencken's invective may now seem (his hilarious but no longer exactly accurate description of the South as "the Sahara of the Bozart," his lapses into mere name-calling: "the 100 per cent, Methodist, Odd Fellow, Ku Kluxer, and Know Nothing") or however dated his targets may have become (Warren G. Harding, Calvin Coolidge, Mary Baker Eddy, Anthony Comstock, Prohibition), one is forced to admit that his indictment still has its relevance and that his intuition of the developing character of American life was fundamentally sound not only for his time but for our own.

Mencken was all on the side of intelligence against stupidity, sophistication against provincialism, excellence against mediocrity. He also fought, and fought vigorously, against all forms of bigotry, censorship, and social oppression. He was as stern a champion of tolerance and understanding as the most militant liberal of today. But he wanted tolerance for enlightened opinions and for an emancipated and more rigorously humane existence, not a tolerance for the third-rate, and certainly not the kind that takes the form of a generalized and uncritical permissiveness. His concern was at all times with standards, with measurements of quality, and he quite rightly feared for the future of standards in a country which, even in his day, was evidently being worked upon more and more by the eroding processes of massification.

It is just here, in Mencken's concern for qualitative questions, that the datedness of his position seems most poignantly obvious. In fact, this whole preoccupation with the decline of standards, the debasement of civilized values, is the one element which more than any other distinguishes the intellectual climate of his age from ours and his attitude toward American life from that of the radical young at the present time. For the young are apparently not concerned with questions of quality in any sense that would have been understandable to Mencken— as such questions might relate to the richness of the cultural environment, the vitality of the intellectual life, or almost any aspect of the sensitive person's involvement with the national experience. In spite of their official preoccupation with individuality and with mystical states of personal consciousness, the young seem to think, even to perceive, almost entirely in collective and materialistic terms. They appear to be most aware not of qualities but of conditions, and conditions as they affect large masses of people rather than individuals, and as they exist in relation to the great bureaucratic institutions of society. For them, virtue or freedom or salvation does not seem to be finally a personal matter at all. It is not to be found in creative fulfillment, in aesthetic appreciation, or in the solitary pursuit of excellence in any form, but rather in the radical revision or overthrow of the existing power structures, in the abolition of a system that seems to them to have manipulated or programed their responses, grossly limited their freedom of choice and action, and generally obstructed their progress toward utopia—which in their view seems to be a condition of infinitely harmonious, democratically depersonalized interpersonal relationships. Thus we hear from the young on almost every conceivable aspect of our educational system, our legislative processes, our foreign policy, and our economy. They tell us that we live in a repressive society, that we keep millions in poverty while fighting a senseless, immoral, and grotesquely expensive war in Vietnam, that our universities are corrupt, and that the instruction offered in them is irrelevant to their needs. But that is about as far as their critical understanding of our predicament seems to go. Although they are highly sophisticated politically and are sensitive to the point of paranoia about institutional injustices and the kinds of problems that might be corrected through procedural reforms and the allocation of funds, they appear to have only the faintest awareness of those other than the procedural that have most to do with shaping the character of the individual life in our society.

One reason for this is that they bring to the experience of their time a political and psychological orientation vastly different from that of earlier generations. Mencken and his contemporaries, for example, based their judgments of American life on strongly individualistic and aesthetic premises. A surprising number of the writers and intellectuals of the twenties and thirties—and even a fair number who reached maturity in the forties—had grown up in the small towns of the Middle West and South and early suffered the trauma of estrangement from a provincial culture which either had no interest in artistic and intellectual values or was actively hostile to them. Hence the pattern of their first relation to their environment became like that of the small boy in Joyce's "Araby," who imagined that he bore his chalice "safely through a throng of foes," or like Stephen Dedalus's proud struggle to survive within the oppressive atmosphere of Ireland. Their only hope was to hold out against the forces of mediocrity, preserve their talents as best they could from philistine contamination, and live for the day when they would be able to escape to a freer and more civilized environment. The classic symbols of escape were the urban East and Europe, to which most of them eventually fled and which gave them the perspective they needed to assess their experience of American life. Their alienation from that experience was, of course, deepened by the very process of judging it by the standards of another—and, in their view, superior—culture. If they were strangers at home, they were doubly strangers *from* home in New York or Paris or London, where they were able to recognize and measure the precise extent to which they did not belong and never could have belonged to the provincial worlds of their childhoods. It was a lonely position and by contemporary liberal standards an arrogant and élitist position. Yet it seems to have been the only one these writers could have assumed at the time, and it helped to make possible the preservation of talents which might otherwise never have developed. Certainly it led to the creation of some of the most vital literature this country has ever produced, vital just because it was written out of a powerfully critical consciousness of the deficiencies of the national life achieved through a direct *personal* engagement of that life by the writers concerned.

And that finally was the whole point and distinction of the radical literary movement of the twenties. It was a rebellion against certain concretely felt evils in American society, and it was carried out by gifted and individualistic men who, although they may have been in very general agreement on the conditions to be attacked, were in no sense operating in a collective, political, or programatic way. For the chances were that each of them had had his own particular experience of these conditions, had suffered because of them in a particular social environment during the most impressionable period of his life, and therefore saw them in specifically human, rather than generalized institutional, terms. The subjects to be exposed or satirized in the books these men came to write were those which, if they were typical, they remembered having personally and traumatically confronted in the real Winesburgs, Zeniths, and Gopher Prairies in which they grew up—the hostility to culture, the emotional impoverishment, the moral hypocrisy, the Babbittry and Boosterism, the emptiness or ugliness of the physical surroundings, the absence of civilized amenities. In short, the objects of rebellion were the direct outgrowth of experiences painfully lived by a generation of writers who were still able to have a vital relationship with the *specifics* of American life, even if it was an enormously abrasive relationship, even if their involvement with that life was the result of the very intensity of their alienation from it.

But this sort of relationship, and the essentially qualitative, antimaterialistic, and environmental approach it was based on, became in the thirties a luxury which the deflated economy could no longer support. Because of the Depression and the profound social and psychic dislocations that followed from it, questions of quality came to seem frivolous in the face of the practical urgencies of existence. The ideological emphasis shifted from a concern for standards to a concern for conditions, from a critical preoccupation with the sterility of small-town and middle-class life to a compassionate preoccupation with the economic plight of the underprivileged. And since for very different economic reasons (primarily the emergence of a state of affluence that has revealed to us the gross inequities of a system which the Depression revealed to be merely unstable) the underprivileged once again occupy the center of our attention, these interests dominate our view of American society far more completely than they did even in the thirties. In fact, our thinking at the present time has become so firmly fixated or petrified at the level of social problems and utilitarian solutions, and such a quantity of free-wheeling self-righteousness has been mustered in support of them, that the concerns of Mencken and his contemporaries must seem not only dated but positively subversive of the most sacred tenets of the liberal philosophy—as indeed, given our humorless and guilt-stricken view of that philosophy, they unquestionably are.

This shift of emphasis has been especially noticeable in the intellectual community, perhaps because all revisions of doctrine tend to occur there under conditions of high evangelical fervor. But American intellectuals have traditionally taken upon themselves the double function of monitoring the national social conscience and upholding aesthetic standards, of policing by turns the moral and the cultural landscape of the country. During times of relative social stability, their concern for standards becomes dominant, and they then attack the culture because it is vulgar and anti-intellectual and fast sinking into the swamp of kitsch and drek. During times of social instability or inequity, their liberal sympathies emerge: they forget standards and begin fulminating against the oppression of the masses. Hence, both during the Depres-

sion and at the present time, they have operated primarily
as critics of the social and economic system, and today
they are championing the same causes and calling for
the same reforms so boisterously urged by the radical
young.

The result is that the young lack recourse to an authority which might instruct them in the reality of qualitative
questions at the same time that they also lack the kind
of specific and concrete relationship with their environment which would give them an independent sense of
such a reality. Because they grew up in an environment
both unappetizing to look upon and too disinfected of
tension and risk to engage them personally, and because,
unlike Mencken's generation, they do not derive their
cultural values from Europe, they have never known what
it is like to fight the battle of the provinces, nor have they
been exposed to another culture against which they could
measure the aesthetic deficiencies of their own. From the
beginning they have belonged to a mass society existing,
for the most part, in uniformly tasteless, suburban middle-
class surroundings, and they have apparently always regarded themselves not as sensitive and superior individuals but as members of a large and homogeneous
group whose principal distinction seems to be that everybody in it agrees with everybody else. In fact, they must
be the first generation in history to see itself from the
outset as a herd rather than as an aggregate of private
persons who happen to be the same age. Consequently,

instead of feeling separate and aloof from the masses and contemptuous of the concerns of the masses, they identify psychologically *with* the masses, and so quite naturally conceive of the world's salvation in collective terms.

It follows logically from this that, as I suggested earlier, the better life for them is not to be found in the development of the self in spite of, or in opposition to, society but rather in the transformation of the structures of society, a transformation which they seem to believe will enable everyone to live in a state of continuous ecstatic togetherness. It is also logical that they should not find very much reality in the idea of individual excellence or care about raising cultural standards, if only because higher standards would work a hardship upon people too incompetent or lazy to meet them—and that, of course, would be discrimination.

In a sense, what has happened is that the pieties and prejudices of the mediocre—which were legitimate targets for ridicule in Mencken's time—have been assimilated into American social thinking at all levels and given moral authority by the liberal establishment. The idea that all men are, or ought to be, equal under law or in the eyes of God has been adulterated, out of the purest motives, into the notion that all men are equal in every respect, and that differences among them are either illusory or the result of the inequitable distribution of wealth and opportunity. Thus we have the peculiar phenomenon of apparently sophisticated and certainly

49

high-minded idealism for the reform of society existing side by side with the crassest and most philistine views of the nature of man in society. The rationalizations of the old booboisie have evidently been reincarnated in the clichés of the Old and New Left.

Nevertheless, the political and social aims of the young must seem altogether admirable when one considers them in the abstract and ponders the almost heartbreaking faith in human goodness which they represent. We may require radical, even sweepingly visionary proposals for reform in order to make certain that small modest improvements will eventually be made. But little will be gained by the adoption of their proposals if the quality of the national life and of the individual life is further diminished in the process, if the erosion of standards is allowed to continue, if the environment is increasingly ravaged and uglified, and if the poor are liberated from physical poverty into the far more wretched poverty of mind and spirit which is the typical middle-class condition at the present time.

5.

As I have suggested, the failure of the young to ask qualitative questions—or at least to be concerned about them with anything like the intensity they display toward political issues—seems to be the result of their lack of vital relationship with their physical and cultural surroundings. They cannot, after all, be expected to have a very clear sense of the quality of their environment if they have never seen it except as an abstraction or as a neutral medium of mass action, and do not bring to it aesthetic expectations by which they could gauge its aesthetic inadequacy. If, on the other hand, they had ever found themselves in conflict with a strongly resistant environment or had access to any of the older, more provincial, and more readily engageable forms of social confrontation—with the small town or neighborhood, with authoritarian parents or overly strict discipline at school—they would have found their environment real, and the question of its quality crucial, just because they existed in a state of constant opposition to it and suffered within it, as Joyce suffered in and so found real the life of Dublin, and Thomas Wolfe the small-town life of the South. But it is difficult to imagine how one can confront or resist an environment which puts up no resistance, which is open, bland, uniform, monotonous, and at the same time smoothly functional and accommodative like that of the modern housing development. All one can do with a housing development, besides live badly in it, is find it too dull and depressing to be noticed. If a person has grown up in one—and in America over the past twenty years a child of the middle classes could scarcely have avoided that calamity—it would not be surprising if his sensibilities were as atrophied as the optic nerves of fish spawned for centuries in caves.

In any case, this same abstractedness from the environment may also be the reason the young are so obsessed with broadly procedural and political questions, with abstract social issues rather than with the concrete specifics of social experience. They appear to think habitually in terms of collectives such as establishments, bureaucracies, systems, and power structures, and they do so, it would seem, because they have little or no direct contact with the realities which compose these institutions. In a sense, they are preoccupied with methodology, with the processes of manipulation and negotiation, because they see such institutions as remote and dehumanized entities to be pressured or propitiated rather than as organizations of real people who have specific personal interests, the usual mixture of greed and benevolence, as well as real problems which might obstruct the processes of instant reform.

Of course, one recognizes that this is simply a condition of life in a mass society. We have grown accustomed to existing incommunicado as part of a nameless mass, or inhabiting a nameless structure containing a mass, rather than being individual people with individual names and voices. Perhaps for those of us who are older the problem is not so serious, because after a while one develops little pockets of personal life where one can withdraw and temporarily escape the mass. But the young have very little sense of a personal life and an overwhelming sense of a collective life. In fact, they have been obliged to make a group metaphysics out of a social necessity. They are collective first and personal last, in both their thinking and their behavior, because the conditions of their existence offer them no other alternative. Yet this does not lessen their frustration when they are confronted with the Kafkaesque remoteness of an authority they want personally to reach and, if they fail to reach, to provoke through collective action into some kind of human response. They will naturally act in such a way as to create a conflict which the authority must either resist or find means to resolve, for in so doing they are trying to force the authority to acknowledge them as trustworthy agents of arbitration or as enemies with whom arbitration is impossible—either of which roles would, of course, be preferable to that of passive existence in a vacuum of noncommunication.

To understand the pattern of this relationship to authority, one could do worse than consider the kind of relationship which seems to have existed between the great majority of the young and their parents. With due allowance for the hazards of generalization, it does seem to be true that parents are characteristically seen by the young in very much the same way that they see the institutions of our society—as remote and abstract entities who are neither reachable as human beings nor readily engageable as authorities to be defied and, if possible, overthrown. The average liberal middle-class parents of the fifties and sixties were almost certain to have been more militantly permissive than dictatorial, more guilt-ridden and therefore more doubtful than domineering. They seem to have operated on the assumption that children could be persuaded to do what one wished them to do if one reasoned with them—or, if reason failed, they could be negotiated with and either outmaneuvered or bribed into submission. The result was that their children at a very early age became past masters of the art of political relations and quickly learned how to outmaneuver their parents. This gave them their very strong interest in procedure, in the ways and means by which people can be brought to do one's bidding not only in the home but in the world at large, where they have simply converted the lessons learned at mother's knee into a program of political activism. If parents could be so easily and successfully conned, so could institutions.

This early training also gave the young their sense of *we* versus *them,* their understanding that *we,* with all righteousness but no real power on our side, must skillfully contrive to obtain the satisfactions due us in life from those who have the power, and that these satisfactions take the form of favors granted and rewards offered after some agreement acceptable to both sides has been reached. Getting what one wanted therefore became a matter of putting oneself on the receiving end of largess dispensed from *above* by some charitable agency rather than a matter of personal achievement, the cultivation of one's inner resources, or working cooperatively with the agency concerned toward some common goal. Hence the faith of the young in the ability of institutions simply to take measures, make reforms, and distribute concessions, when properly persuaded or pressured, would seem to be the direct outgrowth of this childhood exposure to the techniques of the welfare state as practiced in the home.

But it should not be forgotten that the parents themselves inhabited an adult society which functioned according to the same laws. Perhaps the satisfaction of their wants did not depend quite so baldly upon the benevolence of some outside authority. Yet they belonged to an age which believed implicitly in the notion that life is a problem to be solved, and that solutions consist of finding the right techniques and creating the right material conditions. In short, their vision of the good life was one which was finally realizable within the system and within the procedural structures provided by the system —through legislative and programatic action and the acquisition of higher incomes, bigger houses, better cars, and more goods and services. Or their problems could be smoothed away through the application of psychiatric therapies, which were merely scientifically organized forms of negotiation and manipulation operating at the psychic rather than the socio-political level.

It was probably no more than natural that parents committed to such a way of life would not, as a rule, have a very firm grasp of problems which do not lend themselves to material or manipulative solution or which might not be open to solution at all. They would scarcely be in a position to instruct their children in the unpopular but necessary wisdom that man is innately weak and imperfect, that human progress is slow and may even be illusory, that political systems cannot always be depended upon to cure the world's ills, that measures cannot always be taken, and that sometimes the most serious problems a man may face are those that exist between himself and his courage or conscience. It may be that the parents did not teach their children these things because they had so little awareness of what they themselves lived for and should live for, because their own lives seemed to be so totally determined by externals. They may also have been too much concerned with the problems of their children to give them a sense of the reality of their own problems. Certainly they seem to have given their children very little sense of their own reality as living and suffering human beings who just possibly might once have had, and might even still have, souls. And because they did not, their children have grown up with apparently no awareness of, or tolerance for, human limitation, and no understanding of the obstacles that may stand in the way of the changes they are so anxious to bring about in our society. They think today in morally purist and naïve terms perhaps because they have never experienced the impurities of the human condition, as those impurities might have been represented to them by their parents. If, for example, their parents had given them a legitimate and useful function in the household instead of allowing them to believe that they were privileged guests, if they had been made to work for their pleasures, or at least been required to wait for them, they might not be quite as dogmatically certain as they now are that solutions must come at once and are given rather than achieved, that virtue is legislated or enacted upon mankind from above rather than earned, often at great price and over a long period of time, from within.

6.

These expectations, and the almost laboratory purity of the influences that shaped them, make the behavior of the young in the universities remarkably easy to predict. One can count on them to demand instant answers to very complicated questions, to be more preoccupied with ways and means than with ends, and to feel precisely as estranged from the university authorities as they felt from their parents. Even the corporate nature of their rebelliousness is beautifully in character for a generation accustomed from the cradle to thinking, acting, loving, and hating in unison. Yet there is something about the very predictability of the whole performance, especially its quality of seeming so evidently to *be* a performance, that is both puzzling and a little ominous. One has the sense at times of witnessing the enactment, and the incessant re-enactment, of an initiation ritual which once had important meaning for the race, but which in our day has lost its sacramental power and hardened into a mere histrionics of confrontation. Traditionally, in primitive ages, the vital feature of the initiation ritual was that it was to be enacted and *passed through*. Its value lay in its being a phase in the process of human growth, a climactic moment in the transition from adolescence to adulthood. The tribal or parental authority would grant, or refuse to grant, the young initiate membership in the adult community depending on his success in meeting the tests of manhood— his power symbolically, not only to challenge the father but eventually to overthrow him and take his place. But the interesting thing about the current version of the ritual is that it is emphatically not looked upon as an application for membership in the adult community. It does not seem to represent an effort to overthrow the father or his institutional surrogates but simply to challenge him and them and, if possible, to prolong the period of challenge into a lifetime. Like frieze figures on a Grecian urn, the young of today seem to be arrested forever, and to have chosen to be arrested forever, in their stance of confrontation, and to view with horror the prospect of passing beyond it.

One of the obvious and much-documented reasons for this is that the experience of university life is itself no longer looked upon as a phase of initiation to be passed through. In fact, the sharp change in attitude on this one point probably accounts more than anything else for the misunderstanding that now exists between the current group of campus militants and their elders. Where the older generation took it for granted that universities were essentially training schools in which one developed the intellectual skills and served the intellectual apprenticeship required for entry into adult society, the young appear to see them as microcosmic representations *of* adult society, embodying in peculiarly concentrated and virulent form all the bureaucratic evils of the social system as a whole. Hence, where our impulse was to be graduated as quickly as possible so that we could begin to fight what we imagined to be the battles of real life, their impulse is to defer graduation as long as possible in order to fight the battles of the campus, which for them *are* the battles of real life.

Nevertheless, it would seem that the universities are far more real to the young as combat areas of political challenge and confrontation than as institutions requiring specific reforms. Although the necessity for reform is the ostensible and conscious reason for their protests, one notices how vague the militants are about the precise nature of the measures they wish to be taken, how much more articulate they are in their demands for confrontation than they are about the concrete issues of confrontation. Sometimes it does indeed seem that, except for the violently radical minority who wish to see all institutions overthrown just because they are institutions, most of the militants are interested in the act or ritual of protest simply for its own sake and as an end in itself, and one cannot help suspecting that they would be wholly frustrated and outraged if some of their more extreme demands were ever actually met.

This may seem paradoxical, but the underlying psychology is clear enough. The young come to the universities with little or no respect for their parents, hence little or no respect for adults in general, and very little experience of organized adult authority. At the same time, their lifelong exposure to parental overprotectiveness and permissiveness has given them a massive respect for themselves and an absolute faith in their own authority. But the trouble with their own authority is that since it has never been opposed, it has never actually been tested. It has evolved in a vacuum of nonresistance in which wants were satisfied by peaceful negotiation rather than through a direct or violent contest of wills. Thus, however convinced they may be of their authority, they have not had the chance to discover just how authoritative it is, and the universities provide them with that chance on a grand scale. Through challenging the authority of the universities, they measure the strength of their own, and so long as the challenge can be maintained—and to be maintained it must be constantly escalated—their own authority is in effect maintained, if only because their sense of their own power and importance derives so largely from their function as unrelenting moral monitors of the educational establishment.

The response of the young to resistance from the establishment is ambiguous but again perfectly understandable on the psychological level. If and when their demands are opposed, as they are bound now and then to be in even the most liberal and conciliatory institutions, their immediate reaction is anger: first, because they are unused to opposition from adults; second, because opposition jars, however momentarily, their belief in the instant perfectibility of the world; and, third, because anger is the basic ingredient of their stance as a social group as well as the index of their moral superiority. On the other hand, opposition delights them because it confirms the opinion they have long jealously guarded that adults, where not absolutely feckless, are by nature and reason of their spiritual corruption, reactionaries, if not fascists, at heart. But they are delighted also for another and far more crucial reason—because if adults can be made to resist rather than equivocate or compromise, the young will at last have achieved a condition they have never known in their lives before, and that is vital both to their psychic health and to their solidarity as a group. They will have found something to push against and form themselves in opposition to, something their parents did not give them and which they unconsciously blame their parents for not giving them. But it is extremely important, as I have said, that the opposition be sustained. For a continuous state of tension and confrontation not only allows them to preserve their authority but provides them with the means of crystallizing their sense of identity, which is at once a feeling of dramatic connection with their social environment after years of being abstracted from it and a feeling of being real persons set apart from their environment by unresolvable differences. It also, of course, feeds their self-righteousness, of which they have gargantuan quantities, by allowing them to believe that they are engaged against heavy odds in a noble struggle for moral freedom.

Thus the young have very large vested interests in keeping alive the tensions between themselves and adults, and they take care to do this by making progressively more radical and unreasonable demands upon the universities, demands which they know perfectly well will not be met—or, at any rate, which they hope to God will not be met. The beautiful part of the strategy is that it can be continued indefinitely. Regardless of the concessions the universities agree to make, the young can always be outraged because they were not made earlier. If a dozen reforms are instituted, there are always two dozen more that ought to be. In short, there will be grounds for confrontation forever, even if they have to be invented. The important thing is that the show must go on. There is much too much at stake to allow it to close. In fact, quite simply everything that gives the young their distinctive character is at stake—their smugness, their moral superiority, their righteous indignation, their sense of togetherness, their politics, their religion, their vocation, and their avocation. For so long as the delicate balance of tensions is maintained, so long as the young continue their fight but contrive by clever manipulation never quite to succeed in winning it, their status and security as a generation are assured. But if all their demands were ever met and a negotiated peace finally arranged, they would have no choice but to merge their identities with that of the establishment and work within the authority of the establishment. They would then cease to be the generation especially appointed by the Lord to lead the world out of the pit of iniquity and would become simply anonymous junior members of the corporation. This would not only represent a woeful violation of their moral principles but would cost them the protection of their collectivism. They would be forced to leave behind the cover and concealment of their mass crusade, in which all values and issues have been defined for them by the bureaucracy of the mass will, and to begin to make their way on their own as separate, solitary, and terribly vulnerable individuals. They would have to begin to think for themselves and

65

compete for their identities on the open market of adult society, and that, as I have suggested, is a fate too horrible for them to contemplate.

The kinds of demands the young make on the universities are notable for two reasons: first, because so many of them are simply escalated forms of the expectations of personal freedom created in the young by their parents; and, second, because they are so largely procedural in nature and relate not to the life of the mind but to methods for organizing and conducting the life of the institution. For example, one of the more popular demands at the larger universities is that students be allowed to choose their own curricula and have a major voice in determining which will be the courses required for a degree in a particular field of concentration. It is possible to sympathize with any student who wishes to have some control over the content of his education, particularly if he suspects, often quite rightly, that his education is in the hands of cretins. But one ought also to be aware that the notion of educational self-determination is a perfectly logical outcome of a childhood experience in which few or no restrictions were placed on the child, and parents habitually made it a point, in moments of choice, to let the child cast the deciding vote. Such delegation of authority occurring at an early age is hugely flattering to the young ego and is conducive to either megalomania or a wonderful independence of mind. Unfortunately, very few children are gifted enough to derive high intellectual strength from this sort of freedom. The great majority are conditioned by it to become capricious, self-indulgent, and drunk with the glory of their incontestable omnipotence. Thus they enter the universities convinced that whatever is required is wrong. Any exercise of authority, any imposition of laws, is a violation of their civil liberties as well as their divine rights as members of the new royal family of adolescence. It is also a violation of the rules of the game they have been playing all their lives, the particular variety of checkers in which they were always given the first move and allowed to jump backward and forward on the board long before they had earned any kings. Hence the demand that they be allowed to create their own educational programs is a demand simply that the universities continue the practice of delegating to them the authority which was first delegated to them by their parents, to allow them to do as they please simply because it is *they* who please, even if they are not yet educated enough to know whether what they please is right. But behind it all, of course, the process of probing for the limits of adult permissiveness continues, and must continue, to operate. For not even the most thoroughly spoiled child actually believes that the game will always be played on his terms and to his advantage, nor does he desire that it should be. His sense of his own identity and authority, if it is to be real to him, requires a sustained dialectical relationship with an adversary. Restrictions on his freedom must be found and the pressure of opposition to them kept constantly at a high pitch of intensity.

The equally popular demand that university instruction be made "relevant"—relevant, that is, to the problems and issues of immediate contemporary concern to the young—is closely related to the demand for educational self-determination and is also rooted in the childhood experience. To understand this, one needs to recognize that the most crucial problem facing the promiscuous reproducers of the forties and fifties was the problem of keeping the child from being bored to death. This required unremitting vigilance and a high degree of ingenuity on the part of the mother, and forced her to seek constantly for distractions which the child would accept as "relevant" to his whims of the moment. Whenever existence threatened to become routine or in the least deficient in the creature excitements, a bribe or reward immediately pleasing to the child had to be offered to prevent him from going berserk and distracting the mother from her own distractions. One did not pursue a difficult or monotonous task because it might eventually prove to be interesting, or was interesting precisely for the reason that it was difficult, or because the final result might be eminently worth working for. One at once sought relief from it because monotony and difficulty were unpleasant, and everyone had long ago agreed never to find life unpleasant.

Equipped with this sort of lotus-land metaphysics, the

young arrive on the campuses with a very low boredom threshold and a very high expectation that their courses, functioning as mother-surrogates, will keep them safe from boredom by providing distractions that will seem compatible with their current interests. They naturally approach their courses with the belief that the burden of proof is on the course and not on them. Like Mummy, the course exists in a state of perpetual probation. It must prove itself worthy of engaging their attention and, if possible, of exciting their enthusiasm, and it must do this by demonstrating its relevance. If its relevance is not immediately apparent, if it does not provide them with insight into the problems of the ghetto, the politics of Chicago, or the corrupt leadership responsible for the Vietnam War, then obviously it must be replaced with something that is either more fun or more readily convertible into their intellectual currency.

Of course, the very idea of judging education by the standard of its relevance to the concerns of adolescents is childish, for it is the child who can comprehend the world only to the extent that he can see it as an embodiment of, or source of satisfaction for, his infantile desires. An adult should be able to extrapolate from the personal to the general and find meaning in ideas which may have only the most tangential relationship to his particular feelings and experiences. But the most obvious arguments against the demand for relevance—that the young are not yet old enough to know what is relevant and what is not; that what may seem irrelevant at twenty may seem ferociously relevant at forty and fifty; that monotonous and routine learning is sometimes necessary if one is to master a discipline such as language or mathematics and so be in a position to judge its relevance; or that routine learning may simply be good for one, good training for the mind, good training in the joys of work; or even that the question of relevance is itself irrelevant if one shares the view of most educators that all knowledge is relevant because all knowledge is related, in the sense that it is coherently formed out of the accumulated life experience of the race—these arguments, since they derive from a concept of deferred gratification, can only seem meaningless to a generation resolutely in pursuit of instant gratification and accustomed to evaluating knowledge on the basis of its utility value or its topicality in the area of current events.

It is just here, in their pragmatic approach to knowledge, that the young reveal what must be the most ironical and, for them, the most embarrassing of the many inconsistencies underlying their position. For although they profess to be vigorous opponents of technocratic society, anti-materialists to the core, and ardent believers in the primacy of feelings over things, states of soul over states of physical affluence and well-being, their idea of relevance happens to be a perfect expression *of* technocratic philosophy, which evaluates knowledge on the basis of its usefulness in solving practical problems and in providing statistical measurements by which social phenomena are analyzed. It would seem, therefore, that the thinking of the young has been programed by some of the very influences they are rebelling against, and that in their crusade to restructure university education in the shape of their interests, they are in fact giving aid and comfort to their supposed enemies. But this may not be so very surprising when one considers that they have all along displayed an inordinate interest in procedural questions and answers, and that even their interest in feelings and soul, like their infatuation with tarot cards and Eastern mysticism, is not so much a sign of religious consciousness as another form of their search for mechanistic solutions—in this case, a kind of easy-to-assemble, do-it-yourself metaphysics which, once constructed, will "explain" or cure the complicated problems of being and function as an occult welfare program for the spiritually underprivileged. Thus one can see how the young would be obliged to take only a very slight tuck in their thinking in order to move quite happily into the brave new world now in the process of being created by technocracy, a world in which all problems will be solved by social engineering, all injustices erased by benevolent legislation, and all qualitative values declared irrelevant—very probably by law.

Part Two

7.

One cannot observe the student activist drama for very long without beginning to feel, with Marianne Moore, that "there are things that are important beyond all this fiddle." At one time, we would not have needed to be reminded what those things are. But after nearly a decade of activist fiddle and at least two decades of being brainwashed by the doctrine that whatever is young is right, we have become ashamed to admit a truth we once thought too self-evident to need stating: that universities are not primarily rebel encampments, forums of political debate, or media for thé distribution of pamphlets, but institutions whose first function is to train intelligence and preserve cultural standards.

It is perfectly true that historical precedent exists, particularly in Europe and South America, for both the activist and the educational roles of the universities. Very often in the past, students have served as indispensable agents of public conscience, using their relative freedom from the pressures of expediency and compromise to impress upon the adult world the reality of moral issues on which there must be no compromise. But almost always in the past the two roles have existed in some sort of balanced relation to each other, and except in times of the most extreme ideological crisis, the one did not usurp, eclipse, or threaten to vitiate the authority of the other. Today, however, the activist role has become so inflated in our universities, and the educational role so diminished where not downright subverted, that we now accept it as customary to find students whose function on the campus is primarily that of agitation and only marginally that of becoming educated. Obviously, there are serious and intelligent students who are dedicated to activism. But since we can hardly assume that the many thousands or even millions of young people now engaged to one degree or another in campus agitation are *all* serious or intelligent enough to be dedicated political idealists, we must presumably seek elsewhere for an explanation of their behavior.

In the Country of the Young

In addition to the reasons I have already offered—the rather complicated psychological motives for confrontation, the need, among other things, to oppose, and be opposed by, adult authority in order to define personal identity—one might suggest that the present college population is so constituted that many of its members are bound to be drawn to activism simply because they are suited to no other role. This is, after all, the first student generation to be admitted to the universities on the principle that higher education is a right that should be available to all and, at the same time, a necessity for anyone who hopes to achieve some measure of success in middle-class society. The result is that for the first time in our history the universities have had to accept large masses of students who may have proper credentials from the secondary schools—because those schools have themselves been obliged to lower their standards to accommodate the mediocre majority—but who possess neither the cultural interest nor the intellectual incentive to benefit from higher education. Such students, when confronted with complex ideas or stringent academic requirements, tend to sink into a protective lethargy or to become resentful because demands are being made on them which they are not equipped to meet and have no particular desire to meet. Most of them did not want to come to the universities in the first place but did so for reasons of practical expediency: parental pressure, fear of the draft, or the promise of a better job after graduation. But these motives, since they are imposed from without rather than generated from within, are not sufficient to sustain them through the rigors of their course work or give them a sense of purpose inside the structure of the university. Hence their natural impulse is to try to compensate for their failure of ability or interest by involving themselves in some extracurricular activity, which happens today to be political activism.

This kind of involvement has at least one important advantage over involvement in football and fraternity life: popular opinion has sanctified it as a worthy, even a heroic, cause. Students with only marginal interests in anything else can therefore give themselves up to it not only without feeling guilty or frivolous but with the pious conviction that they are doing something far more valuable—and certainly far more "relevant"—than training their minds, and something also which requires no special talent or mental capacity beyond a certain talent for indignation and the power to be vigorously inarticulate while trying to express it. Thus they are afforded moral justification for not doing what they do not want to do and, at the same time, an approved outlet for hostilities resulting from the pressures that are exerted upon them to do what they are not readily able to do. Besides, engaging in attacks on the universities is the surest strategy for deflecting criticism from themselves. Whatever failure they may be charged with they can blame on the institution and thereby convert their sense of individual inadequacy into a far more comfortable sense of collective self-righteousness. Finally, of course, activist participation has the advantage of guaranteeing students the approval of their peers—a measurable status within a university community as a rule so large that a person would normally be lost in it—and the privilege of feeling socially effective, which is a rare privilege for the socially ineffective.

But perhaps the most crucial factor of all is simply the boredom of the vast majority of students, a boredom which must be at least equal to, if not considerably worse than, that of the population as a whole. Without strongly internalized ambitions and interests that are satisfiable within the university system, average students, like average people everywhere, are entirely dependent upon outside stimuli to provide them with the distractions needed to make life bearable. The greater the intellectual vacuum, the greater the need for distraction, a vacuum in people being presumably even more abhorrent than it is in nature. Thus run-of-the-mill students are especially vulnerable to the enticements of activism as well as to those of its soul-brother philosophy of hippyism. Activism supplies them not only with abundant opportunity to be active without having to think but with a sense of concrete physical involvement in a kind of experience from which normally they feel rather tragically excluded. Here, after all, they are: young, vigorous, hairy, horny, not terribly bright, and aching for murder, and all the great occasions for challenge and adventure seem to have passed them by. They were born twenty years too late to have a part in that knightly crusade against tyranny which World War II now seems sentimentally to symbolize for their fathers. They did not even have the small but appealing satisfaction of going hungry in the Depression. And, to make matters worse, the only available war is one they cannot morally accept and which they would consent to fight in only under the gravest duress. Obviously, there is a vacuum here more insidious than an intellectual vacuum, an absence of the opportunity for therapeutic bloodshed, and for the really imperative confrontation between man and his fear of death.

The virtue of activism is that it provides a fair substitute for this lost opportunity. It restores the primitive connection between belligerent virility and a hostile environment, and, in so doing, makes it possible for the young to get a little of their own back from history. It allows them to fight their own morally acceptable war, carry on their own knightly crusade against tyranny, in brick-throwing street battles with the police and in stalwart confrontations of nerve with authorities old enough to be as enviably favored by history as Dad. They can taste blood in these encounters, and they can taste fear, and with a little luck they can contrive to become martyrs and spend a night or two in jail. The police may not be entirely satisfactory replacements for the Nazis (although there are differences of opinion on this score), but they can be as easily charged with brutality as the

universities can be charged with corruption, and so can
be conveniently transformed into enemies one can hate
with a clear conscience and attack whenever one needs
proof of one's courage or relief from one's boredom.
Through activism, in short, life can become once again a
frontier and a battlefield. The bland abstractedness of
university life is canceled by violence and melodrama,
and those who cannot function effectively on the frontier
of ideas are brought back into touch with a reality they
can understand.

The main difference between activism and hippyism—
at least where the question of their attractiveness to the
young is concerned—seems to be that hippyism appeals
to an even more feckless and intellectually empty sector
of the student population than activism does. In other
respects they are very much alike, particularly in the
respect that both offer powerful distractions from boredom and even more powerful rationalizations for that
sensation of being without identity and purpose which
afflicts so many mediocre students in the mass university
society. If activism flatters the mediocre by allowing
them to believe that their search for distraction is really a
heroic political crusade, hippyism similarly flatters them
by allowing them to believe that their ineffectivity is in
fact a serious metaphysical position and connected in
some portentous way with the power of positive feeling,
courageous individualism, and the mystical wisdom of
the East.

Thus the hippy notion of complete freedom to do your own thing in your own way is attractively translatable into the notion that to be accepted by the group you don't have to have very much of a thing or be able to do very much with it. All that matters is that it is your own and *you* are doing it. Hence you are free, and respected for being free, to be your own limp and aimless self. The ego dividends, furthermore, are enormous. In doing your own thing you are performing an act of spurious creativity and individuality entirely without cost to yourself. You are emulating the artist while enduring none of the agony and needing none of the talent of the artist, for the stipulation that you can do as you like relieves you of the necessity to produce anything interesting or important. The act is totally onanistic. It is for your benefit alone. Therefore, if doing your own thing happens in your case to be doing nothing but listening to your beard grow or sitting under a tree and plucking that old guitar or some other equally meditative activity, that is perfectly all right.

The hippy interest in uninhibited feeling has very much the same kind of appeal. Feeling, after all, is a private affair. Nobody can be sure what you are feeling or if, in fact, you are feeling anything. Also, the etiquette governing hippy feeling requires that you not talk about it or express it except in a grunt or almost any intestinal noise signifying ecstasy. Your only obligation toward feeling is to feel it. But the person of defective emotional equipment or limited vocabulary is protected on all counts. He does not have to describe what he feels, so if he feels nothing, nobody is the wiser.

This philosophy, when applied to sexual feeling, yields similar protective benefits. The hippy doctrine of more or less random, free-for-all sex would, of course, appeal irresistibly to any normal raunchy adolescent who has harbored the dream of one day discovering a paradise in which he could have a quick lay whenever he felt like it without having to worry about the girl or feel anything beyond the joy of ejaculation. Suddenly, under the copulative offices of hippyism, he is at least theoretically allowed to do just that, and, what is even more delightful, he is allowed to do it on the very best of all possible moral terms. He can tell himself that while indulging in this form of coital masturbation he is actually performing a service to bourgeois society by helping to liberate it from its repressive sexual attitudes, and even that in the enjoyment of his freedom he is attaining oneness with the Infinite, God in this case being, to update James Joyce, not a shout but a screw in the street. Thus all the major pieties of the hippy moral canon—personal freedom, defiance of social convention, the sacramental nature of orgasm—are marshaled to the support of the urge for erotic anarchy among those of the young who have nothing on their minds but their groins.

It is also interesting to notice how much of the attraction of hippyism derives, like that of activism, from its power to provide an outlet for the nostalgia felt by the young for a past they were born too late to experience. If activism gives them an opportunity for violence and a sense of heroic mission emulative of the more adventurous moments of history, hippyism allows them to affect the manners and costumery which have become identified with the life styles of past ages. Thus one sees the hippy young wandering the streets dressed in the U.S. Army tunics of World War I, in the broad-brimmed hats and plunging sideburns of the Western plainsman, in the headbands of Comanche braves, in Edwardian suits, the smocks of French Bohemian painters, or the gaudy saris of guruland.

One supposes that in itself there is no particular harm in this sort of masquerade. The young need to have something to do with their banality. But its social and psychological implications are depressing in the extreme. At the most serious level, it is obviously meant to represent an act of rejection of the modern age and a declaration of preference for drama, individuality, and romance. The World War I uniform is presumably cherished as a sacred relic of a war fought according to the principles of a now debased idealism. The Western plainsman, with or without his sideburns, enjoyed the distinction of being a loner, a law unto himself, the master of his manhood, and of using his strength in honorable contest with the primitive forces of nature, a kind of contest no longer possible in the denatured society of the present time. The Indian, of course, was the original American frontier Negro, the first victim of our corrupt bureaucratic system. He was also our first innocent, happy and free in his native Eden, until the white man conquered and brainwashed him so that he would be content to live miserably on a reservation. To emulate him is not only to remind the establishment of its ancestral guilt. It is to suggest that the young, too, were once happy and free like the Indian, and might have remained so if only they had been left alone by adults to do as they pleased.

All this is understandable, if rather infantile regressivism. But the sad thing is that as a form of defiant self-assertion it is so singularly impotent, so utterly without force or originality, so lacking in the power to make a critical or even satirical point or disturb in any serious way the complacency of those it is supposedly intended to provoke. As social protest, it is empty because it offers one kind of futility in ostensible rebuttal of another kind of futility. If modern life seems meaningless, it is absurd to attack it by resorting to an even more blatant meaninglessness. Walking around in the exhumed costumery of another age is no more interesting or daring than capitulating to the system and becoming a General Motors slave. In fact, the truly radical gesture these days would be to do just that. But both have equally little relation to the problem of how to achieve real identity and individuality in the modern world.

Yet this is undoubtedly just the point: the hippy young have no interest whatever in achieving real identity, and the only individuality they seem capable of is a most curious kind shared by thousands of others to all appearances exactly like themselves. This corporate, ready-to-wear idiosyncrasy is clearly their means of evading for as long as possible the trauma of self-confrontation and the attendant trauma of finding themselves gazing into the pit of their own bottomless vacuity. So long as they enjoy the camouflage of interchangeable sartorial décor, they will be protected from all encounters with the real and with the self. They can become as children and exist forever in that state of fantasy in which children dress up in the clothes of their parents and in so doing imaginatively take on the awesome mystery and glamour of adults. But these particular children would not be caught dead in the clothes of their parents, for the variety of death they most abhor is adulthood. They prefer to remain at the stage of development where role-playing, the amusing charade of the nursery, is an end in itself, and where, through the costumes they put on and take off, they can make and remake imaginary selves, secure in the knowledge that nothing they do is real, that life is a fiction, that all is as it appears to be, and everything appears to be something else.

8.

All that I have said here may seem to be accurately descriptive only of the dullest and least accomplished members of the student population. They are logically the most susceptible to boredom as well as sufficiently uncritical to be taken in by such mindless entertainments as hippyism. Yet any sort of close contact with the young soon convinces one that the tendencies dramatized so flamboyantly by the mediocre can also be found among many of their more gifted and intelligent contemporaries, whose distinction is perhaps that, being smarter, they dramatize them not flamboyantly but with a kind of leaden self-righteousness. But mediocre and gifted alike appear to share the same compulsive need for diversion and excitement, the same indifference, if not downright hostility, to ideas, the same horror of adulthood, the same obsession with procedural questions and material solutions, and the same desire to inflate the role of student into a lifelong professional career.

It is a common experience in the universities to find students who, regardless of their capabilities, have absolutely no notion of what they want to do with their lives, and to whom the idea of doing anything beyond what they are already doing is tainted with the foul smell of compromise and therefore of corruption. Integrity for them appears to consist in the infinite refusal to commit themselves to any program of action that might challenge their moral presuppositions or force them to leave behind the protective sanctity of studentism. The worldly ambitions of earlier generations to become doctors, lawyers, businessmen, or artists—and to become the very best possible—are, of course, still occasionally to be found. Regressivism even among the young is not always infantile. But such ambitions are rare and they are suspect, because as a rule the young are frightened both by what they consider the arrogance of any aspiration to excellence and by the likelihood of having sooner or later to scale down whatever aspiration they may have in order to meet the requirements of expediency, the practical limits imposed by life and human weakness. It seems to them better not to aspire at all, and thus keep one's idealism intact, than to aspire in the face of almost certain compromise and be forced to settle for something less than absolute fulfillment. Their need for instant gratification demands that success be guaranteed before they will consent to try for it. Hence it is the usual thing to find them describing the future in terms of self-protective negations and their plans for the future, if any, in terms of strategic withdrawals and postponements. One will try after graduation to go to Europe for a year and look around; one will apply to the Peace Corps; one will hitchhike out to Berkeley and do a little demonstrating and street-fighting; one will contrive to stay forever in graduate school.

It is easy to understand how anyone in his right mind might hesitate to embrace the joys of adulthood in a time like the present. The options open to the young for the pursuit of an adventurous or productive future may not actually be, but do certainly seem to be, far more limited than they were, and the chances are very good that before one has had time to discover what they are, one will get killed or maimed in a meaningless war. This is no country for young men right now, and it has never been a country for old men. But the failure of a sense of future in the young is not the result simply of adverse conditions peculiar to this age. They also suffer the handicap of having formed their impressions of adulthood very largely on their parents, and it is obvious that the example of their parents has in most cases given them little except strongly negative attitudes toward the possibilities of adult life.

To the extent that they are certain of anything at all, they appear to be in agreement on one point: they do not want to become like Mother and Dad. The prospect of settling down in a dull job and a dull house, working to pay off the mortgage, seeking identity in reproduction and then living for the children—with all that this implies in boredom, self-sacrifice, and generalized atrophy of the soul—fills them with a special kind of terror. Yet their experience of their parents has given them very little understanding of what the alternatives to this sort of life might be, and very little impulse to create their own alternatives. The best they seem able to do is lose themselves in their own form of middle-class anesthesia and live in the hope that some benevolent catastrophe will destroy adult society before they are obliged to enter it.

A large part of their problem is that their relation to both their parents' way of life and the social environment in general has been so lacking in abrasiveness that they have not been impelled to create their identities through opposition or insubordination. If, as I said earlier, this deficiency has given them a singular indifference to questions of quality and an overriding concern for procedural problems and material solutions, it has had an even more crippling effect on their power to think independently about the future and to initiate the kind of intensely personal rebellion *toward* the future which can only result from an intensely personal rebellion against a restrictive past.

Thus it is not enough for the young simply to feel alienated from the way of life of their parents and to have no wish to emulate it. They must be *productively* alienated, in the sense that they are stimulated or provoked into wanting to create for themselves a more vital and meaningful way of life. Unfortunately, the trouble with their particular form of alienation is that it is too complete to be productive in this way. It involves apparently a breakdown of understanding, sympathy, communication, and even mutual hostility so total that they are simply abstracted from their parents' world altogether and left stunned by the utter incomprehensibility of everything their parents represent. Hence, the effect of their alienation is not liberating but stultifying, because it closes out every opportunity for effective connection with the home environment, and in particular the kind of connection that is produced by overt conflict. The generation gap is thus, contrary to middle-aged opinion, far more damaging to the young than it is to their parents, for the psychic health of the young can well depend on their being able to communicate with their parents, even if communication consists of shouting and screaming at them, so that the young themselves can, if they so choose, create the gap on their own initiative and discover such freedom as they can in that ritual stroke of umbilical surgery. But when they are deprived of this possibility, the young tend to fall *into* the gap and to flounder there in a state of bewilderment, or they will simply desert from adult society without ever having belonged to it or declared war on it, and spend their time seeking ways—and usually the most insipid ways—to tranquilize their feelings of confusion and ineffectuality. For their need is, and must always be, to reach their parents, to be able to identify with them or do battle with them, and in so doing to define themselves.

This is to suggest that if the young had encountered genuine resistance from their parents, if their mothers had been strict disciplinarians rather than meekly permissive and their fathers had been domineering, bigoted, and hypercritical, thus becoming figures of real influence, however negative, on the lives of their children, there might have been some real ground for confrontation, some palpable force to defy or overthrow. But the parents of this generation were evidently so often bland, tolerant, well-meaning, and anxiously solicitous of their children that the only possible response to them was one of indifference or sad contempt, neither of which offers a very sound basis for rebellion, self-definition, or even a usable Oedipus complex.

Such a basis has, of course, been provided to some degree by the universities, which represent for many of the young their first contact with a structured and potentially resistant environment, and therefore their first opportunity for the kind of confrontation denied them by their parents. But the trouble with the universities is that they provide this opportunity too late in a young person's psychological development to benefit him to any important extent—so late, in fact, that it more often than not does him important harm. By the time he has reached university age, he should ideally have already formed the emotional and intellectual premises on which he will create his place in adult society. He should already have acquired the wounds and frustrations needed to propel him toward some goal of personal fulfillment. He should already have begun to convert his hostilities into determination and his sense of inadequacy into an ambition to excel. But if he has had to wait until university age to encounter an environment that will generate these compensatory impulses in him, he is likely to become arrested in the role of perpetual confrontation and reconfrontation of authority because his experience is, in effect, forcing him to regress to a stage of development which is inappropriate to his age. Instead of being free by that time to use the facilities of the university to train his mind and prepare himself for effective adulthood, he is compelled to use the university as an arena for the enactment of the parent-child conflict he never had, for getting rid of aggressions which he should have got rid of or learned how to turn to his own emotional advantage years before. Thus the opportunity for rebellion provided the young by the universities is essentially an opportunity to remain adolescent, to carry forward the missed rebellion of their childhoods, and while so doing to stay safely within the benevolent protection of the institution, to make a fetish of concern for the deplorable conditions of university life—in the hope, of course, of making them seem repressive enough to deserve being rebelled against —and to exist in such a fever of indignation over the evils of adult society that they will seem morally justified in not joining it. In a very real sense, the child is indeed the father of the man, and if the child does not have a chance to father the man at the right psychological moment, he is likely to remain a child forever.

9.

It is nothing new to say that a little material hardship would also have had a liberating effect on the young. One does not wish to reanimate that ancient cliché with which self-made men used to browbeat their indolent sons, the one about getting up before dawn, milking six cows before breakfast, and walking four miles through hip-deep snow to the little red schoolhouse. This is our mythic apprenticeship for greatness, but it has turned far more fathers into sanctimonious bores than it has created heads of state. Yet the human organism is so constructed that, if left undisturbed, its natural tendency is to lie under a tree all day and pluck that old guitar. Some pressure of necessity or irritation, whether external or internal, is required to get it on its feet. It must hunger, thirst, lust, itch, or aspire, come into some abrasive relation with either its physical environment or its guilts, before it is motivated to go to work. Thus the children of affluence and permissiveness have a double problem. They have been emotionally as well as intellectually impoverished because the irritant of necessity is missing from their physical environment and the irritant of guilt is missing from their psychological environment. They have been so heavily indulged by their parents, have been the recipients of such massive quantities of every kind of unearned largess, that they feel no need to ingratiate themselves with their parents in order to win their attention or approval. They already have more approval than they can stomach simply by virtue of being the marvelous creatures they are. If there is a burden of proof or a reason to feel guilty, it belongs not to them but to their parents. They are the ones who must earn the approval of their children, for they, after all, bear the responsibility for having caused the children to be born into this dreadful world, and that is an offense for which no amount of atonement is excessive. In addition, they have caused their children to grow up with a sense of economic security so complete that the traditional obligation to do something or become something seems downright anachronistic. In the opinion of the young, it is absurd to spend one's life worrying about money when there is obviously so much of it around. And if parents continue in the face of this fact to spend their lives worrying about money, that only proves the truth of what the young have all along been saying: that the older generation has been corrupted by materialism and has lost touch with the things of the spirit, which, of course, can only be properly appreciated if one is relieved of the necessity of having to worry about money.

The great virtue of economic depression is that it combines a very low degree of opportunity with a very high degree of motivation. It creates limits within which one is forced to function, and in cutting down the range of available choices it dispels the confusion about where best to apply one's energies. One *has* to apply them only where conditions permit, and one has to apply them in order to stay alive. Hence one takes the available job, and in time that job may become a career and an entire way of life. But if the pressure of economic necessity is missing, not only is motivation reduced to a minimum but one is confronted by such a plethora of possibilities for using one's energies that one may become paralyzed with indecision and end by doing nothing at all—or, like mice in an overly complicated maze, turn psychotic and simply sit down and goggle at the wall.

This is the kind of paralysis afflicting so many of the

97

young at the present time. Affluence and their relative freedom from the motivations of guilt have allowed them to view dispassionately the possible choices of career open to them and to have very little compulsion to choose one over the other. The choice, if it is to be made at all, must be made more or less arbitrarily, as if they were trying to decide between two identical glasses of sour milk. They must simply pick a career and say to themselves that that is what they will do with their lives; if they have to become something, they might as well become that. Such an attitude is not likely to produce ambitious men, and it is certain not to produce dedicated men. What it does produce is a college generation and a young professional generation whose concern, when they select a career, is all with externals, who make a certain choice because it will enable them to live in California where they can go skin-diving, or because it provides high fringe benefits, or, in the case of teaching, because it offers security and long vacations. Their deepest interests, their most basic psychological drives, are not involved at all—indeed cannot be involved, since their work is neither an extension nor a vindication of themselves. They are not called, chosen, or compelled but are simply working because they are obliged somehow to fill up their time and get paid for it. Hence they fill up their time not in making original contributions to their fields, not in the creative investigation of ideas, but with the busy work of professionalism. They camouflage their lack of genuine involvement by serving perpetually on committees, by becoming experts in the art of political intrigue, by analyzing the administrative policies of institutions, by showing extravagant concern for the methodology, but rarely the content, of university instruction—by engaging in the trivial backing and filling that represents the diversion of the intellectually uncommitted.

It is perhaps fortunate for such people that affluence has produced a particular social etiquette which tends to discourage self-fulfillment and to promote self-effacement. The uncommitted young are naturally obedient servants of this etiquette, and it is not surprising that they have inflated it into very nearly the proportions of a new world religion—since whatever their ineffectuality impels them to do, they are inclined first to make holy. But one notices that as the economic and psychological pressures to distinguish themselves from others—whether through aspiration or achievement—have declined, new pressures are being exerted among the young to enforce cooperation with others and deference to the feelings of others. Subservience to the interests of the group has come to be regarded as the supreme virtue as well as the most valuable attribute of the ideal society, while competitiveness of any kind, like intolerance of any kind, is considered very bad form indeed and may result in one's expulsion from the group. To be gentle and unassuming, to be solicitous of one's peers and sensitive to the delicate shifts of their emotional temper—in particular, to project an image of oneself as having no personal being apart from the being one shares with others and which is their communal property before it is your private property—all this is to be not merely humane but to affirm one's membership in the universal brotherhood of man, which enfolds us all in a warm placenta of togetherness and makes us one flesh and one soul.

This philosophy, shorn of its undergraduate mysticism, obviously has its origins in the childhood experience of the young. From a very early age, they have been accustomed to manipulating and negotiating with just about everybody they came into contact with—friends, parents, baby-sitters, teachers, and university administrators. They have always belonged to a massified society in which skill in social politics was an imperative of survival and the frictionless interaction of groups far more important than the needs and desires of any individual. The emphasis for them has therefore always been on being well-liked, well-adjusted, and cooperative—not well-adjusted simply in the usual sense of the word but well-adjusted to whatever the fashionable maladjustments of the group might be at any given moment, and cooperative not just with one another but in their group refusal to cooperate with the older generation. They have been programed from the beginning to think in collective and procedural terms, and the reward available to them has been the reward customarily available to those who serve obediently: the tender feeling of being accepted into and approved by the fraternity of the mass. Individual achievement or any difference from others in personality, behavior, or dress would, of course, be dangerous because it would place barriers of inequity between oneself and others, and that would offend the collective mediocrity. Thus it follows that even the radicalism of the young and their bizarreness of appearance and manner are the products of their conformity to the mass will, their inability to respond to the experience of their time in an individual way. But then their philosophy decrees that individuality is wrong; therefore its absence is not a psychological defect but a moral virtue.

The rather cloying interest shown by the young in the phenomenon known as "communication" has its significance here. Communication is an experience which they value particularly highly not only because it is the ultimate expression of their other-directedness but because it frees them of the necessity to raise themselves above others through individual achievement. If you are devoting your energies to trying to communicate with others, you are obviously not able to devote them to self-fulfillment. Your psychic eye is turned outward rather than inward, and you are counting on an intimate relationship with another person to supply you with the gratification you would otherwise be forced to create through the solitary cultivation of your own resources. Besides, the two interests are political opposites. The desire for self-fulfillment makes for unpleasant competitive tensions between people and is by nature aristocratic, since it presupposes that what you make of yourself is more important than what you make with others. Communication, on the other hand, democratizes in the sense that it necessarily takes place between people who wish to share themselves with each other and who are therefore equals rather than egotistical snobs. Hence if you have no particular ambition to fulfill yourself or suspect that you have very little self to fulfill, it is a great comfort to be able to rationalize the deficiency by insisting that reaching others is actually far more socially valuable than self-fulfillment —that, in fact, it may even be the *highest form* of self-fulfillment.

It is also comforting that the kind of communication most favored by the young just happens to be the non-verbal kind, which can neither be described nor objectively evaluated. You can say that you are communicating with someone, and it is impossible to prove whether you are or not. The whole thing is beyond the power of mere language, and, of course, it is so beclouded by specious religiosity that to question it would be as gross an infringement of the right of worship as asking the devout to demonstrate the efficacy of prayer. Either you believe in it or you do not, but you are not required to put it into words or formulate its meaning or its message rationally. To communicate in this way is to employ meanings that do not need to be articulated, meanings that one simply *receives*—especially if there are no complexities of thought to interfere with the transmission. It is all a matter of soul speaking to soul, lovers passionately sweating skin to skin, blown minds exchanging psychedelic mash notes—non-thoughts floating in non-words between nonentities.

10.

All this may help to clarify one of the most fascinating paradoxes underlying the psychology of the young: the contrast between their collective vociferousness and their individual inarticulateness, their public militancy of manner and their personal limpness of manner. This is an incongruity which causes everything about them to exist in double focus and to take on more than a little flavor of high black comedy. It seems logical to assume, for example, that the violence of the obscenity-screaming, brick-throwing student mob would be a fairly reliable indication that the rioters are people of violent temperament whose aggressive behavior as a mob accurately reflects their aggressive character as individuals. Yet all it appears to signify is that the young are schizoid. For once away from the barricades, most of them behave so very differently that one suspects that their public belligerence has no relation whatever to their real natures but is simply a kind of ferocious costumery they put on in order to play a convincing role in the generational hostility rites. Apparently, they have a manner, just as they have various items of peculiar clothing, which they consider it appropriate to wear on ceremonial occasions, and another manner which they keep for everyday, and the two are as dissimilar as the faces of Eve.

In ordinary circumstances, when they are not operating as a Tartar horde, the great majority of the young seem to be creatures of remarkably flaccid personality. One senses in them a singular blandness, even a temperamental nullity. Where tics and crotchets ought to be, one finds vast reaches of spiritual moonscape, cold, sunless, as vacant as space. Talking to them is rather like talking into an electronic box that takes messages for people who are not at home. Part of the problem is that so many of them are so entirely without self-consciousness and idiosyncrasy that it is immensely difficult to get any clear impression of the person behind the face. It seems that the fashion now is to have not a face but a façade, a décor personality to go with the décor costumery and consisting of features that are equally standardized. But where the costumery is at least flamboyant, the personality is so colorless that one is obliged to describe it almost entirely in negatives. It is possible to say that it tends to be basically insensitive, often as if under some kind of sedation; intellectually untidy, perhaps because the capacity or the paranoia required for intellectual precision is simply not there: frequently discourteous, although seemingly more out of abstractedness than any specific urge to be rude; as lacking in grace and guile as a child of two, yet poised, relaxed, urbane, and always completely self-assured. There is as much surface presence and internal absence in the type as one would expect to find in the most promising junior executive at General Motors. The electric, tense, exacting, cantankerous, abrasive, ambitious, and obsessively self-monitory personality so characteristic of past generations of rebels seems to have become as obsolete as the fat boy and the freckled-faced redhead with warts, and one very, very seldom encounters any longer a young person who is sufficiently maladjusted as to be shy, or who appears ever to have known what it is like to blush or tremble with stage fright when required to perform in public. The acting experience comes early these days, and whatever else the young may or may not be, they are the most confident and accomplished troupe of public performers in our history.

106

In the Country of the Young

Their style of delivery is as much a piece of standardized décor as their style of personality. It may be that we have achieved, after years of painful evolution through steadily widening gyres of unselective breeding, a mode of speech that is the precise verbal expression of our democratic heritage. But the young have carried the evolutionary process forward—if that is the correct direction—into yet another phase, and, in so doing, have inevitably increased the number and variety of resources on which colloquial American is able to draw for its linguistic materials. The result is that their speech is a sort of patois of most of the major sounds ever uttered by human lips within their hearing: Mississippi Negro dialect, Appalachia hillbilly, the jargon of technology, the jargon of political science, the jargon of psychiatry, the jargon of the ghetto, the jargon of rock-music culture, the jargon of the dope addict, and the jargon of Madison Avenue—to name only those that come first to mind. Americans—perhaps because they have become deranged by the babble of so many parochial tongues—have always been the most lingually sloppy and tone-deaf people on earth. Listening to them talk, particularly after one has been away from the country long enough to have stopped taking the sound for granted, is like listening to parrots just coming out of ether. Our women are famous throughout the world for having voices which seem to proceed from some vengeful agitation of razor blades immediately behind the nose. And just as this sound must be symptomatic of some atonality of soul, the slack and derivative speech of the young seems to be the perfect idiom of their fecklessness.

Of course, it takes no special knowledge of human psychodynamics to understand why the young are this way. If they are people of notably limp personalities, it is very probably because certain factors necessary to the development of strong personalities are missing from their experience. This is to say that strong personalities, like all neurotic disorders, are made rather than inherited, and they are made, as a rule, not by conditions of jolly good fellowship, such as are enjoyed by the masses of the young, but by conditions of a far more stressful kind.

Essentially, it would seem that the factors required for strong personality are the same as those required for strong ambition: some degree of psychological isolation at the right moment in life and some productive relationship with an accessible but resistant environment. To define himself, to become aware of himself at all as an individual human being, a person needs to acquire what Henry James called the perspective of "otherness." This can only be acquired if he has the opportunity to be physically alone for extended periods during adolescence, and creatively alone in the sense that he is deprived of the usual social distractions and soporifics, and therefore is forced to turn inward and seek satisfaction in the consciousness of his own powers, the cultivation of his own unique perceptions. In time, if the isolation is prolonged, a person will develop a powerful awareness of his own identity and a correspondingly powerful awareness of the very different identities of other people. He will take on the spectatorial attitude, the habit of seeing what is happening in the world of others as interesting or remarkable or preposterous just because it is happening to them and not to himself, because they are strangers or actors performing a play in which he has no part. It may even be that the role of the spectator is essential in a very basic sense to the development of perception, for conceivably we see only to the extent that our eye is attracted by the incongruous and unusual. If nothing within the range of our vision seems remarkable, we are likely not to notice it at all or we may simply register it unconsciously as normal and therefore as forgettable. On the other hand, the greater our sense of the incongruous, the greater will be our effective range of vision, for we will be like children perpetually seeing the world as if for the first time. Freudian psychology suggests that intelligence begins when the individual begins to separate himself from his environment, when through psychological isolation he ceases to perceive his environment as merely an extension of himself—and so, it seems, does personality begin.

But the state of isolation, however valuable it may be for a certain period, is neither desirable nor supportable if continued for too long a time. It can only lead to permanent withdrawal, a distortion of the perspective of otherness into a sense of estrangement, and eventual im-

mobilization of the psyche. Luckily, the tendency of
healthy people is to try sooner or later to break out of
their isolation and achieve some kind of productive
relationship with others by impressing their personalities
on them, perhaps through idiosyncrasy, emotional
warmth, intellectual excellence, or creative accomplish-
ment. It is necessary to confront the human community
and to make use of the energy or wisdom acquired in
isolation to earn one's membership in the community or
to define one's differences from it. But for this to be
possible, the social environment must be accessible, and
it must also be at least initially resistant. It must put up
barriers which will stimulate one to impress one's personality upon it and try to subdue it. This is why access
to the small, provincial environment such as the neighborhood and town, or to an oppressive home environment,
is so necessary to vital rebellion, just as it is necessary
to the creation of vital personality. One is goaded into
self-definition by the pressure exerted by the environment
to force one into conformity.

But the problem for the young is, as I have suggested,
that so many of these essential influences are missing
from their lives. They are, above all, a generation which
seems never to have been alone; hence they have never
endured psychological isolation or been compelled to
develop the perspective of otherness. The experience of
the small, provincial environment is as historically and
culturally remote from them as the English country-

house life portrayed by Jane Austen, and they most assuredly show no signs of having suffered from an oppressive home environment. To most of them the social world has not been an arena of personal confrontation or conflict but the very embodiment of irrelevance, for they have always known the vast, vacant, structureless world of modern suburbia, which it is impossible to identify with and even more impossible to rebel against, which does not encourage the spectatorial attitude or provide one with a sufficient sense of incongruity even to see it as effectively *other*. Everything about it conspires to make one wish not to see it, to make one turn away from it, but turn not in to the self—since that would only complete the process of estrangement—but frantically outward to the society of one's contemporaries. For it is undoubtedly because they have been unable to identify with the physical character of their social environment that the young have identified so completely with one another and sought in the society of one another the sense of human connection denied them by their environment. In fact, it would seem that the society of one another *is* their only accessible social environment, their only medium of satisfactory social experience.

Thus it follows with sound Darwinian logic that their personalities should be perfect adaptations to the requirements of the collectivist society which they inhabit, that they should be self-effacing, colorless, politic, and free of all competitive tensions and idiosyncrasies. They have

111

not needed to prove their worth or compete for the approval of the group because approval is instantly granted as a condition of generational membership. They have not needed to develop themselves intellectually because the group does not believe in ideas, only in actions. They have not needed to learn how to express themselves in language because the group has learned how to communicate without resorting to language. They have never felt estranged from one another, only from everybody else, so there is no question of their ever having had to impose their personalities upon their environment in order to provoke or subdue it. They already *are* their environment—and it is perhaps not a sufficiently militant irony to daunt their deadly earnestness that their qualities of personality are remarkably similar to the qualities of their physical surroundings, that they are just as bland, vacant, and structureless as the drek culture with which they cannot identify but which now seems to have reclaimed them, as the jungle sooner or later reclaims even the most domesticated of its creatures as its spiritual brothers and human counterparts.

11.

All this bears rather strikingly on the character of their rebellion, and they do rebel, of course, if only to determine whether they are as irresistible to strangers as they are to one another. But it seems evident that if the young display individually little or none of the aggressiveness they display collectively, the reason must be that their emotions are not engaged by the issues which they collectively support, that there is something impersonal about their public anger and programatic about their zeal for reform. They are demonstrating, it would appear, in the name of abstractions and theoretical constructs of issues rather than the concrete specifics of issues, and one supposes they are doing so because they lack direct personal experience of those issues, because they are precisely as detached from the world in which those issues literally exist as they are from the realities of their social environment.

This is to say that their activism seems to be the result more of ideological commitment than of direct personal frustration and suffering, and perhaps that is why they cling to it so passionately—because it is what they have instead of personal involvement, because it is a structure of ideological intensity which has all the appearance of feeling without having been derived from feeling, and so is their only means of confronting experience in a dynamic way. They are very probably the first generation of American rebels not to have suffered to some degree personally as a result of the injustices and inequities which they seek to eradicate, and this has created a crippling separation between their principles and their emotions, between their official idealism and their practical understanding. If they had ever actually been the victims of privation or persecution, if they had ever known the ugliness of discrimination, lived among the poor of Appalachia or Harlem, gone hungry, fought in a war, or tried to survive under Russian or Chinese Communism, they might have found a living basis for their outrage and discovered the terms of an effectively personal rebellion. They might also have found a corrective for their tendency to romanticize the masses as well as the joys of life in a Socialist republic. But affluence, American citizenship, and their favored or unfavored position in history have deprived them of these experiences and so left them physically and psychologically isolated from the objects of their official compassion and anger, theoretical in their concern for other people's realities.

This quality of abstractedness is revealed in the oddly obscure vocabulary they use to describe the evils which they wish to overthrow. They talk compulsively and ritualistically about "power structures," "systems," "establishments," "bureaucracy," and "technology," and the vagueness of these words, their failure, when used singly, to describe specific conditions in a real world, is symptomatic of their function as empty pejorative metaphors for problems not personally engaged by those who use them. It almost seems that such language is intended to invent a reality, or to lay false claim to the existence of a reality, which the young can then attack—as if they lack an objective correlative for their sense of grievance, sufficient justification for their impulse to revolt. By the same token, they appear to be far more interested in being militant about these verbal abstractions than they are in working to correct conditions that do have objective existence. They will demonstrate against "technology" but do nothing to help the technologically un-

John W. Aldridge

employed; against "oppression" but do nothing to help the real victims of oppression, who are most certainly not themselves; against "power structures" but do nothing to curb the abuses of their own power structure, which is rapidly becoming the most powerful and bureaucratic of them all. But the point, of course, is that the unemployed and oppressed are unreal to the young because they are outside the range of their specific experience, while the abstract catchwords of their dissent, the Newspeak of the very technology they profess to hate, give them the only sense of connection they have with experience beyond the society of one another. It would seem that to the abstracted only abstractions are real, just as modes of procedure are more real to them than concrete goals, and the administration of universities is more important than the content and quality of the ideas generated within them. Clearly, the young are suffering from a massive dissociation of sensibility, a loss of relationship with the living realities of the world. And the fact that such connection as they have with experience is so largely theoretical and verbal, as tenuous as the language on which it is based, may be the best evidence we have that their crusade represents not so much a vital engagement of imperative issues as a failure on their part to cut through the opaque tissue of their rhetoric to the real dark center of American life, where, if they could keep their courage, they might encounter provocations worthy

116

of their outrage and learn the right names for whatever forces may be tyrannizing us.

It may be that it is just this isolation from the specifics of the national experience which has given the young the impetus for their rebellion. It may be that their militant actions represent an effort to bring about a confrontation not with authority but with reality, the kind of face-to-face confrontation they have been unable to achieve in any other way. But it is one of the many sadnesses of their predicament that their search for reality leads them inevitably back to authority, since, given their isolation, there is nothing else for them to confront. They are locked into the programed circuits of mass bureaucratic society to such an extent that even their rebellion must be carried out within them. Just as technology can only be described and attacked by the young in the language of technology, so power structures can only be opposed by the erection against them of new power structures, those of revolution becoming finally as repressive of individual freedom as those they are intended to destroy.

But a far more poignant irony lies in the fact that the vision of the future so widely shared by the young is also the result of technological programing. For it would appear that their isolation from the specifics of experience inside the bureaucratic cage has given them such a horror of experience that they have incorporated into their image of the ideal society precisely the bureaucratic restrictions they now find restricting, and so project a society purified of risk, uncertainty, and every form of physical and intellectual challenge, the aim presumably being to make life safe from every possible intrusion of life. Their abstractedness, in short, has caused them to conceive of a paradise of abstractedness, to escalate the nightmare of their alienation into a dream of utopian alienation.

This is, of course, exactly the kind of society that technology has been endeavoring all along to bring into being, and it is a logical extension of the one the young are now demonstrating against. If left alone, our present society will naturally evolve into it, and if the reforms of the young are instituted, it will most certainly do so more quickly. But what is especially interesting is that this is also a more highly disinfected version of the society which their parents created for the young when they were growing up, one in which measures could always be taken and solutions could always be found and happiness consisted of discovering infinite distractions from the real. Thus it is possible to wonder, when they envision a world without risk, whether the young are not in fact expressing their nostalgia for the secure, permissive, and instantly gratifying lost Eden of their childhoods, where every day was Christmas, and Mother and Dad were the Good Fairy and Santa Claus for one brief shining moment before they turned into ogres. Surely the controlled environment which they anticipate for the future and which technology will inevitably provide is not so very different from the controlled environment of the nursery, and it is perfectly appropriate to the child's fear of the dark forces of contingency that seem, in his nighttime imagination, so monstrous and threatening. But these happen also to be the forces that give the adult life its edge of adventure and provide the only assurance we have that life is something more than a bubble of contentment drifting between the security of the nursery and the perfection of the grave.

Apparently, the young are so abstracted from experience and so fearful of adulthood that they find this simple truth either incomprehensible or unbearable. Yet one supposes that a crucial event of adulthood is the discovery of virtue in the imperfect and the unexpected. However disturbing it may be to the emotionally delicate, however obstructive it may be of our progress toward sociological Godhead, there is excitement in the refusal of things to be safe, pure, rational, and predictable. The young, of all people, should know this, since it is because we have problems that they have been able to enjoy the excitement of agitating for their solution. Once they are solved, the young will have agitated themselves out of work and right back into boredom. Yet, paradoxically enough, this most rebellious and borable of generations seems to be excited by problems without believing in them. They may derive their emotional sustenance from them at the present time, but they fail to see any value in them either for themselves or for the race in general, and their first act of legislative business when they come to create the ideal society of the future will evidently be to declare them illegal. Hence they do not understand how there might be very real benefits to be derived from experiences that have nothing to recommend them except the fact that they are imperfect or expose one to uncertainty. There is, for example, that much-excoriated phenomenon of their university careers, the bad professor, whose badness might be their only reliable gauge of what a good professor should be or simply prove so abrasive that some enterprising student will be goaded by it into becoming smarter in the field than he is. If, on the other hand, students are confronted by nothing but good professors, they are likely to become overawed by the proliferation of expertise and go away convinced that the best that is known and thought in the world has already been known and thought. It is quite possible that much of the current boredom of university students is the result of their not having encountered sufficient stupidity in their instructors. Sometimes there is no greater stimulus to intellectual ambition than a good dull mind.

The young also apparently find little exhilaration in those other hazards and dislocations of life which can often prove so challenging. They appear to dislike and to do all they can to avoid encountering people who are capricious, crotchety, intolerant, or just plain bigoted rather than reasonable, understanding, and colorless.

They find no stimulus, regardless of the final cost, in the experience of economic uncertainty, in the risk of getting a girl pregnant, or flunking out of college, or choosing the wrong career, or being absolutely alone and against the crowd just because it *is* a crowd and all those people cannot possibly be right. At the moment, they may seem to be taking their chances with the police, but they are taking them not as isolated individuals, not as rebel-outlaws, but as buck privates in a vast army of righteous orthodoxy whose actions have all the choreographed daring of battle scenes in VistaVision. They are also taking their chances in the name of reforms ultimately aimed at the abolition of imperfection from the earth, the removal of all cause for even their own dissent.

This is not quite to suggest that in order to be worth living life needs to be as dreadful or dangerous as possible. Yet it does seem to be true that difficulty brings more of our essential humanity into play than tranquility does and so heightens our responsiveness to life, in very much the way that disease rallies the body's defenses or the eye works more energetically in the presence of varying intensities of light than it does in an all-white room. If, as T. S. Eliot said, "humankind cannot bear very much reality," it also cannot bear too little. We need the challenge of an untrustworthy and resistant environment to wake us from our psychic sleep and give us again the adrenal charge of panic that kept us alive in the jungle dark. We also need to be reminded, as imperfection and risk do remind us, of the possibilities of renewal, of cosmic surprise, the miracle of the fortuitous in nature. We need to be confirmed in our sense that life is individual and original, that we can dare to be lone guns at the shoot-out, that there is still an alternative to lockstep, some room left on the frontier of becoming.

But if imperfection and risk reopen the circuits connecting us with life, perfection, if it were attainable, would be a state of death, and a desire for it must be a desire to die. The solution of a problem, the eradication of some source of enigma or disharmony, represents one more instance in which we have relinquished our hold on the unpredictable, have capitulated to stasis, because we have entombed in some scheme of order, and so neutralized what was once capable of explosive and vital surprise. We necessarily reduce the possibilities of life in our struggle to make it coherent, and we also reduce the number of areas in which we can effectively engage it. In a sense, we struggle not simply to understand our experience but to solve it so that it will no longer have the power to hurt us. The mystery becomes explicable; the dark is illuminated; we see that the shadow under the trees was not a tiger after all; and we are not frightened any more. But we are also less alive.

The fear of life must be powerful in the young, because nothing enrages them more than imperfection, the innate refusal of people and institutions to die into order, and nothing obsesses them more than the necessity to dissolve ambiguities, rectify inequities, and absorb all extremes into a normative condition of equilibrium. Such a desire, in the service of some ideal of creative liberation, could be heralded as the altogether inevitable and necessary urge of a new generation to free society from its paralysis in outmoded patterns of conduct by instituting new patterns more productive of growth. But it would seem that for this generation the precise opposite is the case. Their desire is apparently not to expand possibility but to contract it, to harness experience in its infinite and disturbing variety, to harness men in their infinite and disturbing individuality, to harness the contingent in the service of the safe—in short, to free society from the oppressions of adventure and make it eventually possible for the race to evolve to a point of security where it will be able to exist without having to suffer the pain of life.

It is only through a profound alienation from the dynamics of experience that the human mind can think in such coldly generalizing abstractions about experience, and I have already suggested that this kind of alienation is especially common among the young at the present time. It appears to be responsible for their tendency to see society in terms of large manipulable masses of people rather than individuals, and to be concerned with issues rather than ideas, with quantitative rather than qualitative values, with political and economic reforms rather than the rehabilitation of the physical and cultural environment. It also seems to have produced in them a narrowing of sensibility, a decrease in emotional and intellectual responsiveness, a passivity in the face of challenge, and a rigidity in the face of the ambiguous. Just as the urban and rural landscape has been uglified as a result of the materialism and environmental insensitivity of the men who exploit it, so personality has become trivialized by this same insensitivity to the qualities of existence beyond the material, by its inability to relate to the world except in the abstract, from the standpoint of social theories and technological programs.

All this is particularly unfortunate because if the young wish to make society over in the image of their idealism, they will need all the force of personality they can muster. They will need quite simply to be exceptional men, exceptional in mind, imagination, sensitivity, and courage. But the praiseworthy effort to provide all men with the opportunity for a decent life—and the social philosophy usually responsible for such an effort—is not always congruous with either the need for or the production of exceptional men. We can attempt to save the masses of people only at the risk of destroying the unique and individual. We can become so concerned about rights that we forget about privileges and responsibilities. In trying to abolish unfair distinctions we can wash out distinction. The quality of life can be diminished for all in the effort to raise the standard of living for all. We can easily produce—and may, in fact, have already produced—a society in which more and more people have less and less, and fewer and fewer have really enough. And, of course, the more we concentrate on providing for the security and sustenance of the whole population, the more sterilized of uncertainty and risk life will become. For a collectivist utopia must above all be bureaucratically organized and efficiently run, and every action must be judged on the basis not of its originality and daring but of its value in promoting the greatest good for the greatest number.

Nevertheless, before the young can create such a utopia, they must somehow manage to become original and daring themselves. If they expect to be the custodians of its conscience, as they have tried to be of ours, they had better acquire some direct knowledge of the specifics of moral experience, and this they cannot do without exposing themselves to hazards rather more potent than those they have so far confronted at the campus barricades. If they expect it to embody a revised and liberated American sensibility, they had first better become men of sensibility. If they wish it to be free of materialism, they had better stop thinking so exclusively in materialistic terms. They had also better begin now to develop human resources to put in place of the abolished materialism, resources which will enable them to survive in a world from which not merely materialism but all imperfections will presumably have been abolished—survive *and* create a civilization that will have the power to

125

preserve the quality of the individual life at the same time that it guarantees the tranquility of the collective life.

Yet this is just where the young seem to be singularly ill-equipped to be the administrators of a trouble-free society, for they have left out of account one vital factor: their own inability to live in such a society without going out of their minds. With no more problems to be solved, with no more injustices to demonstrate against, with no more repressive authorities to confront, they would need precisely the dedication to ideas, the interest in aesthetic values, in creative expression, in intellectual analysis, in the amenities of the leisured, affluent life which their preoccupation with solving material problems has prevented them from developing. Thus, in the long hard winters of utopia, they would have complete freedom to do their own thing and nothing to do but face the vacuum in themselves. They would be able to smoke pot all day and all night, pluck their guitars under every tree, screw on every street corner, and go naked whenever and wherever they pleased. But even the young can be diverted only so long by their diversions, by the soporifics that dull, by the psychedelics that substitute a chemical intensity for a life of meaning. Even the naked body grows familiar in time and becomes one more experience of life which is canceled out, which even the most assiduous voyeur is finally abstracted from, through boredom. It is possible that hang-ups would, in the process, be eradicated, and that would represent the achievement of one of the most vital social goals of the young. People would then be liberated from guilt as well as from imperfection, and be free at last to feel absolutely nothing.

Undoubtedly, a society of this kind would eventually become polarized by two extreme psychological types, both of which would be mutations of types that are now rather familiar. There would be the catatonic, and there would be the berserk: the passive vegetable man and the violent mechanical man, opposites in their modes of behavior but identical in their paralysis of feeling. The catatonic would have ceased long ago to strive or respond, for all irritants would have disappeared from his sphere of consciousness. He would have no needs that were not supplied, no desires that were not instantly gratified. For days or weeks on end, he would simply stare at walls or watch, fascinated, the copulation of insects. Having been relieved of the struggle of becoming, he would exist simply to be. The berserk type, on the other hand, would react very differently to the absence of irritants. He would become nervous and disoriented, would roam the streets with mayhem in his heart and nothing behind his eyes except perhaps a baby-blue look of death. Unable to discharge his hatreds in socially approved skirmishes with the police, he would periodically tear up the pavements and throw bricks through store windows and shout obscenities at the sky. It would be violence for its own sake, in the name of no cause except his need to remind himself of feeling, of the way it used to feel to be alive.

In between these two extremes there would, of course, be the millions of normal people like ourselves, people going about their business as usual, seeing nothing amiss, finding nothing remarkable, being tolerant and forgiving, having learned long ago how to live tranquilly together in this best of all possible worlds.

70 71 72 73 10 9 8 7 6 5 4 3 2 1